DIALECT IN WILTSHIRE

DIALECT IN WILTSHIRE

and its historical, topographical and natural science contexts

MALCOLM JONES and PATRICK DILLON

Published by
Wiltshire County Council, Library & Museum Service,
Bythesea Road, Trowbridge, Wiltshire, BA14 8BS
Director: R. L. Pybus, MA, FLA, FCIS, MILAM, MBIM
1987

Photoset and printed by Redwood Burn Limited,
Trowbridge, Wiltshire

ISBN 0 86080 150 0

Contents

v

Foreword

Comment on south-western dialect goes back a long way: when, in 1640, the schoolmaster Simon Daines sets aside (as he says) "the absurdities used among the vulgar in *Sommerset-shire*, and other remote places, as not worth the nominating..." he doubtless means to include Wiltshire among these benighted regions. At this time, and, indeed, until much later, the sport of dialect-bashing – with a predilection for south-western – was a favourite pastime of the educated, since, as Malcolm Jones and Patrick Dillon, in this scholarly yet very readable book, show us, the English language of these areas had undergone a drastic decline in status from the halcyon days of West Saxon to becoming the conventional rustic speech of stage clowns and clod-hopping country yokels. The nineteenth century, with a more enlightened, if more romantic, view of language, reinstated this variety as respectable – after all, it had been the language of King Alfred – and similar views have prevailed – more or less – since: although there is still a tendency to poke fun at the more extreme forms of dialect – especially perhaps those of the north and the south-west – it is now acknowledged that, behind the sounds, grammar and lexicon of dialect speech there lies a long and significant history which we cannot neglect.

The authors of this book deal deftly with the historical background, but it is not all history by any means. Indeed, its aim is to provide an educated, yet readable, account of twentieth-century Wiltshire dialect in its different forms;

that aim, I believe, has been achieved. The fact that children's dialect is not neglected is especially welcome, and is a stepping-stone for much-needed further research in this field. Place-names, surnames and a variety of others also receive attention.

The study of the richly varied forms of present-day English is, of course, one which is widely pursued in places of education everywhere, but it should also be made a more popular occupation, for all of us have a deep-rooted interest in our native tongue which is virtually innate, and that interest deserves to be satisfied. The authors have taken a valuable step in that direction. I am glad to commend this wide-ranging book, and hope that it may act as an incentive to many more of a similar nature on other dialects.

MARTYN F. WAKELIN

Preface

This study of dialect in Wiltshire was conceived some five years ago when one of us (Malcolm Jones) was invited to contribute to the newly-formed "Downwriter" series of local history booklets. After an initial burst of activity, the work, already grown far too large for such a format, lay dormant for a year or so and was resurrected when Patrick Dillon offered to broaden its content by adding topographical and natural science perspectives. From that moment it became a collaborative project and such merit as it now has is in large part due, we feel, to the combination of our philological and natural science interests, a cross-fertilisation which has been of great benefit to us both, and, we hope the reader will agree, to the final shape of the present book.

Making some particular dialect word always our starting-point, we have attempted to show how a knowledge of natural history or landscape evolution, for example, can inform our understanding of the semantics of the dialect lexicon. Although Malcolm Jones is alone responsible for the philological content of the work and thus most of the material in the early chapters, and Patrick Dillon for most of the topographical and natural science dimensions, it is not now easy for us to disentangle the strands of our respective contributions, particularly in respect to some of the later chapters.

As stated in Chapter 1, the material on which this study has, for the most part, been based, is the mass of published data collected in response to the Questionnaire of the Survey of English Dialects carried out in the 1950s, a fact which makes the present work one of the few to date to be so derived. Discussion of individual dialect words not current since the War, as are, for example, the great bulk of those recorded in the late nineteenth-century Glossary of Dartnell and Goddard, has, in the main, been avoided: the emphasis throughout has been on living dialect and genuine survivals, as opposed to historical dialect and fossilised curios.

It will be apparent to those familiar with Martyn Wakelin's *English dialects: an introduction*, how closely our book in its early chapters follows the lay-out of his, and we are privileged to have had the benefit of the comments of such an eminent dialectologist on our text while still in typescript, and his further consent to write our "Foreword"; it goes without saying, that any remaining or newly-introduced errors are entirely our own responsibility. We are grateful too, for the advice of Norman Rogers, author of *Wessex dialect*, who gave generously of his specialist knowledge of our subject.

We are also anxious to record our appreciation of the enlightened policy of a County Council prepared to publish such a technical work, and more particularly, of the efforts on our behalf of Ted Kelly and John Chandler, and of Mrs. Geraldine Curtis who turned an indescribably complex working typescript into a highly polished final product.

A work of this nature would, of course, be impossible without the dedicated professional help of librarians, and in acknowledging that of Wiltshire Library and Museum Service, we particularly wish to record our gratitude to the Local Studies Officer, John Chandler, and the staff of the Devizes Public Library, who have been tireless in their efforts to obtain even the rarest and most obscure items for our perusal. Special thanks, too, are due to Pam Colman, Librarian of the Wiltshire Archaeological and Natural History Society's invaluable library at the Museum in Devizes, and, indeed, to that august Society itself.

For the suggestion of the very appropriate cover illustration we are indebted to John d'Arcy of the Wiltshire

Record Office. We have been fortunate too, to benefit from the advice of various other specialists including Professor M. Samuels, on the localisation of Middle English MSS, Professor Eric Jones, W. Brunsdon Yapp and Professor W. Lockwood on bird-names and ornithological elements of the text, and Iona Opie on children's lore and language.

We are particularly grateful to Jesse Bailey (who may be seen, incidentally, as a young man in our fig. 16), and Mrs. Rose Rogers (who generously provided anecdotes in our Appendix 3) for agreeing to submit to the somewhat intimidating processes of tape-recording, and without whom there would have been little to write about. Thanks are due also to Joan Jones for producing the first, working typescript, Linda Mitchell for drawing the maps, Liz Setterfield for help with transcribing the plant names, David Hollings for the simplified questionnaire for school use and David Carson, Harold Cory and John Peddie for helpful suggestions in the early phase of the work.

Finally, we would like to thank the following for permission to reproduce illustrations: Edward Arnold Ltd., for a page from the *Survey of English dialects* questionnaire; Martyn Wakelin and the Athlone Press Ltd., for a map from *English dialects: an introduction*; Professor N. Wright and Seminar Press Ltd., for maps from *A word geography of England*; Iona Opie for a map from *The lore and language of schoolchildren*; Times Newspapers Ltd., for a photograph from *The Times* of October 30th 1939; The National Trust, Montacute for a photograph of a plaster panel in Montacute House; Fay Stone for the drawing of the "ooser" mask, the Somerset Archaeological and Natural History Society for "clipping the church", and the Wiltshire Archaeological and Natural History Society for the portrait of Edward Hungerford Goddard and reproductions from nineteenth-century printed works.

MALCOLM JONES   PATRICK DILLON
Wensley, Derbyshire   *Great Shefford, Berkshire*
                        April 1985

The authors

MALCOLM JONES is a freelance lexicographer. He has worked in the Department of Medieval and Later Antiquities at the British Museum and is a medievalist as much interested in the linguistic and folklore aspects of medieval culture as in the material aspects. He was formerly Curator of the Wiltshire Folklife Society's Museum at Avebury.

PATRICK DILLON is a Senior Lecturer in the Faculty of Environmental Studies at Bulmershe College of Higher Education, Reading. Although primarily an environmental biologist, he is particularly interested in multidisciplinary approaches to landscape studies. He was formerly Chairman of the Natural History Section of the Wiltshire Archaeological & Natural History Society.

List of illustrations

Depicted on the cover is part of a 1736 map of West Knoyle in the Wiltshire Record Office (WRO 598).

Abbreviations and special symbols

ABBREVIATIONS

a.	before (of dates).
c.	about (of dates).
D&G	Dartnell, G. E. and Goddard, E. H. 1893. *Wiltshire words: a glossary of words used in the county of Wiltshire.*
DHS	Partridge, E. 1972. *A dictionary of historical slang* (abridgement of Partridge, E. 1961. *Dictionary of slang and unconventional English*, revised and enlarged edition).
DNE	Widdowson, J. D. A. *et. al.* 1982. *A dictionary of Newfoundland English.*
EDD	Wright, J. 1896–1905. *The English dialect dictionary.*
EPNE	Smith, A. H. 1956. *English place-name elements*, 2 vols.
LAE	Orton, H., Sanderson, S. and Widdowson, J. D. A. 1978. *Linguistic atlas of England.*
LG	Low German (see below, "Glossary of technical terms used").
loc. cit.	in the passage cited above (in bibliographical references).
ME	Middle English
MS	manuscript
NWi	North Wiltshire
ODEE	Onions, C. T., Friedrichsen, G. W. S. and Burch-

	field, R. W. 1967. *The Oxford dictionary of English etymology*, corrected edition.
OE	Old English
OED	Murray, J. *et. al.* 1933. *The Oxford English dictionary*, 12 vols with later supplements (cited by date).
ON	Old Norse (see below, "Glossary of technical terms used").
op. cit.	in the work cited above (in bibliographical references).
PNW	Gover, J. E. B., Mawer, A. and Stenton, F. M. 1939. *The place-names of Wiltshire*.
RP	Received Pronunciation (see below, "Glossary of technical terms used").
sb.	noun (in OED entries).
SED	Orton, H. *et. al.* 1962–1971. *Survey of English dialects*.
StE	Standard English (see below, "Glossary of technical terms used").
SW	South-West, South-Western.
SWi	South Wiltshire.
v.	verb (in OED entries).
WANHS	The Wiltshire Archaeological and Natural History Society, Devizes, and its museum and library.
WAM	*Wiltshire archaeological and natural history magazine*, 1854–.
WGE	Orton, H. and Wright, N. 1974. *A word geography of England*.

SPECIAL SYMBOLS

ə	The "neutral" vowel sound heard at the end of the word *comma*, for example.
æ	A letter of the OE alphabet (now written *a* or *e*).
ð	Represents the sound of *th* in, for example, *then* (compare next).

θ	Represents the sound of *th* in, for example, *thin* (compare previous).
3	A letter of the (Old and) Middle English alphabet (now written *g* or *y*).
I	The sound of the personal pronoun, *I*, in RP.
*	Indicates a hypothetical, unrecorded or reconstructed form or sound.
‾	Placed over a vowel, indicates it is long (only used here in OE forms).
→	Changes or develops to.
+	Used to show the two parts of a compound word.

Glossary of technical terms used

ASPIRATED With an added *h* sound.

ASSIMILATION The process whereby one sound is changed
into a similar neighbouring sound under the influence of
its proximity. (contrast DISSIMILATION)

COGNATE (adj.) Etymologically related (for example, of two
words in the same or different languages and with
possibly dissimilar meanings); descended from a
common ancestral language, real (Latin, Old English,
etc.) or reconstructed (Indo-European, Germanic,
etc.).

(n.) A word showing such a relationship to another.

DIPHTHONGISATION The changing of a pure vowel sound
into a diphthong, i.e. a combination of a vowel and a
semivowel, for example: *a → ay*.

DISSIMILATION The process whereby one sound under the
influence of the proximity of a neighbouring similar
sound changes into a different sound. (contrast
ASSIMILATION).

ETYMOLOGY The history of a word's derivation and
relationships with others.

FALSE DIVISION (also METANALYSIS) A process of word-
formation where two words, for example, a noun and an
article, are wrongly divided, and a new "mis-formed"
word is produced, for example, *an ewt → a newt*.

FOLK-ETYMOLOGY A popular mistaken ETYMOLOGY of a word
or phrase usually manifesting itself in an obviously

corrupt analysis, for example, *sparrow-grass* for
asparagus, and *Turkey Snipe* for *Turkish Knight*.

FRICATIVE One of a class of sounds produced in the same
manner and including *f*, *s*, *sh*, and *th*.

GLIDE A transitional INORGANIC sound made while the
speech organs move between one position of
articulation and another, for example, the –*w*– in
bwoys.

GRAMMAR The study of the classes of words, their
inflections, and their relations in sentences.

HYPERCORRECTION An unnecessary correction due to a
misinterpretation, for example, *a howl* for *an owl*,
where (presumably unconsciously) it was felt that *owl*
was a non-standard form showing dropped *h*-, which
was therefore "restored".

INORGANIC Superfluously added, for example, the -*d* in
scholard.

LEXICON The vocabulary of a language or dialect. (adj. –
LEXICAL).

LOW GERMAN (LG) The German of the North German Plain,
Dutch, and Flemish.

METATHESIS The transposition of two consonant sounds, for
example, of *r* and *sh* in *bursh* from *brush*.

OLD NORSE The oldest representative of the North
Germanic languages, attested from *c*.A.D.700; words
are cited in their Old Icelandic form, as this is the most
familiar.

ONOMASTICS The study of place-names.

ONOMATOPEIC Formed in imitation of the thing it means, for
example, *cuckoo*, which "sounds its own name".

PERIPHRASTIC Roundabout, using more words than
necessary. The PERIPHRASTIC tenses are those which use
auxiliary verbs rather than inflections, for example, *he
does sing* rather than *he sings*.

PHONOLOGY The sound-system of a language or dialect.
(adj. – PHONOLOGICAL).

r-COLOURING An often INORGANIC r-overtone given to a

vowel etc., for example, StE pronounces *fork* with a long *o* and no *r* sound, but SW dialect sounds the historical *r* shown by the spelling, and will often give a vowel r-colouring where there is *no* historical *r*. (see also RHOTICITY).

RECEIVED PRONUNCIATION (RP) The non-regional standard pronunciation generally used by many educated British people, and formerly, the only variety of English pronunciation heard on the B.B.C. (Note: this is not the same as the so-called "Oxford accent" which is an affected variety of English pronunciation.) (see also STANDARD ENGLISH).

RECESSIVE Receding, on the wane, dying out before some more dominant feature.

RETROFLEX Pronounced with the tip of the tongue turned up or curled back just under the hard palate.

RHOTICITY The full pronunciation of *r* in every context, e.g. in *cart* and *pear* as well as in *ring*, *tree* and *sorrow*. (see also r-COLOURING).

SEMANTIC of meaning; concerning the development and derivation of the various senses of a word.

SEMI-VOWEL A sound midway between a vowel and a consonant, for example, *w* or *y*.

STANDARD ENGLISH (StE) (also RECEIVED STANDARD ENGLISH) The non-regional type of English (lexicon, pronunciation and grammar) generally used by many educated British people. (see also RECEIVED PRONUNCIATION).

STRONG VERB A verb that changes its tenses by means of internal vowel changes, for example, *sing*, *sang*, *sung*. (contrast WEAK VERB).

VOICED (of a sound) that is pronounced with audible voice behind it, for example, *z*, as opposed to one that is not, termed VOICELESS or UNVOICED, for example, *s*. The process that changes UNVOICED sounds to VOICED sounds is termed VOICING.

WEAK VERB A verb that changes its tenses by means of

inflections; in English this means, in effect, one that adds -*ed* or -*t* in the past tenses.

WORD GEOGRAPHY The distribution of individual words plotted on maps.

1

Historical introduction and sources

In the days of the Anglo-Saxons, known linguistically as the Old English (OE) period, Wiltshire, of course, lay in Wessex, in the heartland of the West Saxons, and because of the political pre-eminence of that kingdom, West Saxon became the most important of the dialects that make up Old English (and the dialect in which by far the greatest number of literary and other texts survive).

By the end of the Middle English (ME) period (c.1100–1450), however, the prestige dialect had become not South Western, the successor to West Saxon, but, with the shift of political power from Winchester to London, the variety of English spoken in the new capital of the unified country of England. Before about 1370, London English had combined features of East Anglian and Essex dialects, but by 1430 this had significantly altered, due to a massive influx of immigrants from the Central and North Central Midlands. It was the resultant written variety of this new amalgam of Middle English dialects, the so-called "Chancery Standard", that was the ancestor of our modern written Standard English (StE).[1]

Mainly because of the preponderant bulk of documents surviving in the West Saxon dialect of Old English, that dialect has a good claim to be considered as the standard language of the period; during Old English times, then, the variety of English spoken in Wiltshire can even claim to be more standard than at any time since! West Saxon is such an even continuum that within it, it is not possible, on dialect grounds alone, to locate texts produced in Wiltshire; there

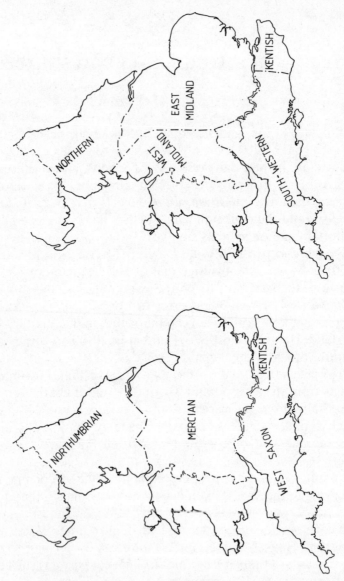

1 *The dialects of Old and Middle English as defined in A. C. Baugh's A history of the English language, 1957.*

2

are, however, a number of Wiltshire land-charters from the Saxon period which are invaluable for the place-names they include, and the evidence of these is adduced in Chapter 5.

By the end of the Old English period and through the early Middle English period the VOICING of initial *f* to *v*,[2] that is now so characteristic a feature of our modern South West dialects,[3] had already begun to take place throughout England south of the Watling Street, though this voicing was later dropped in the South East, presumably under the influence of the more Midland voiced variety of London English.[4] We are fortunate in having at least one very early example from our county: *Fittleton*, near Amesbury, is recorded in *Domesday Book* (1086) in the spelling *Viteletone*, i.e. the *tun* or homestead of a man named *Fitela* (Fitela's existence is confirmed by a mention in a tenth-century charter concerning the bounds of neighbouring Enford).[5]

Apart from such radical phonetic changes which, however, apply to *all* Southern dialects in the Middle English period, not just South Western, recent work by Professors Samuels and McIntoch[6] has established a way of assigning otherwise unprovenanced texts to very precise areas, by means of the careful scrutiny of distinctive spellings of certain common words; two such words are the Middle English forms of our Modern English *given* and *saw*, where the diagnostic Wiltshire spellings are *yȝeve* and *sei/iseiȝ*.[7]

The early fifteenth-century *Life* of the tenth-century St. Edith of Wilton in the so-called *Chronicon Vilodunense* (Wilton Chronicle)[8] is unfortunately not a very good source for the Wiltshire dialect of the late Middle English period; as Professor Samuels concludes, it is "A mixed text, the bulk of the spelling being that of a North Warwickshire man, but with some relics of his Wiltshire original." Instead, Professor Samuels suggests Salisbury Cathedral *MS* 39 (unpublished) as a better text for the study of the Wiltshire dialect of this period.[9] (For further discussion of specifically South Western features in the Middle English dialect of Wiltshire, see Chapter 5.)

In the sixteenth and seventeenth centuries the dramatists often give their rustic characters a stage dialect which is probably intended to be South Western; examples are the language of People in *Respublica* (*c.*1550), and (significantly) of Ignorance in *Wit and Science* (*a.*1550). In *Enough is as good as a Feast* (*c.*1565) Ignorance speaks "Cotswold speech". *Gammer Gurton's Needle* (*c.*1560) is a more thorough-going attempt at a dialect play of this period, but in the seventeenth century the tendency is again towards incidental, humorous, dialect "clowns", as, for example, in the speeches of Puppy (again the name is significant of the lowly status afforded all such speakers of dialect in these plays) in Jonson's *Bartholomew Fair* (1614), and those in his *Tale of a Tub* (1596/7), or of Poor Tom, the madman, in Shakespeare's *King Lear* (*c.*1605. IV.vi. see Chapter 2) in heavy contrast to the standardised language of the Metropolitan court characters.

In 1636, however, we find a sustained and more authentic attempt at specifically Wiltshire dialect in the antimasque prefaced to a masque entitled *The King and Qveenes Entertainement at Richmond*[10] (see extract in Appendix 3).

By the late seventeenth century the collection of dialect words and compilation of dialect glossaries had begun, most notably in John Ray's *A collection of English words not generally used* ... (1674, revised and augmented 1691), which consists of "Two Alphabetical Catalogues, the one ... Northern, the other ... Southern ...". This is also the period that saw the multifarious researches of our foremost antiquarian, John Aubrey,[11] in particular in his *Natural history of Wiltshire* (1656–1691) and *Remaines of Gentilisme and Judaisme* (1686–7), providing us with a fund of mainly incidental information on the Wiltshire speech of this period.

From the late eighteenth century there is the nationwide coverage of Grose's *Provincial glossary, with a collection of local proverbs, and popular superstitions* (1787), and from the middle of that century, the first specifically Wiltshire glossary (the "*Cunnington MS*" in Dartnell and Goddard, *A*

4

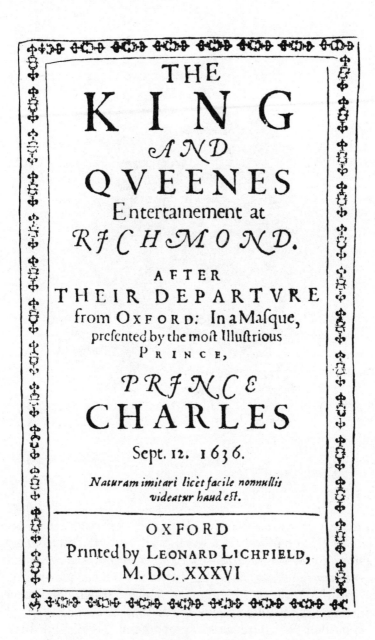

2   *Title page of* The King and Qveenes Entertainement at Richmond, *1636, containing an antimasque in Wiltshire dialect.*

3 *John Aubrey aged 40 in 1666, an engraving reproduced in WAM 4 (1858).*

glossary of words used in the county of Wiltshire (D&G (1893)). Then follow such works well worth the quarrying as Thomas Davis's *General view of the agriculture of the county of Wiltshire* (1794), and John Britton's *The beauties of Wiltshire* (1801), the third volume of which, though not appearing till 1825, included a glossary of Wiltshire words.

Another Wiltshire glossary of about this date (*c*.1811–1828) still unpublished, is bound in the front of one of the Wiltshire Archaeological & Natural History Society's copies

THE

WILTSHIRE

Archæological and Natural History

MAGAZINE,

Published under the Direction of the Society

FORMED IN THAT COUNTY A.D. 1853.

VOL. I.

DEVIZES:

HENRY BULL, SAINT JOHN STREET.

LONDON:

G. BELL, 186, FLEET STREET; J. R. SMITH, 36, SOHO SQUARE.

1854.

---

4 *Title page of the first issue of the* Wiltshire archaeological and natural history magazine *(commonly referred to as WAM), now in its 133rd year and 81st volume.*

of D&G, and deserves to be better known. A few years later comes Akerman's[12] *Glossary of provincial words and phrases in use in Wiltshire* (1842), followed shortly by his Wiltshire dialect stories, *Spring tide*, or the *Angler and his friends* (1850) and *Wiltshire tales* (1853) (see extracts in Appendix 3). The following year saw the first volume of the redoubtable *Wiltshire Archaeological & Natural History Magazine* (*WAM*), where the word "archaeological" was interpreted liberally enough to include matters of dialect and folklore; indeed, this very first number contained a discussion of the "skimmington ride" (see Chapter 8). This focus of antiquarian researches was intensively quarried, together with all the foregoing sources mentioned, and oral testimony, by Dartnell and Goddard[13] in their authoritative *Glossary of words used in the county of Wiltshire* (1893),[14] commissioned by the English Dialect Society, and one of the major sources used in compiling the *English dialect dictionary* (EDD) (1898–1905, reprinted 1981. The *English dialect grammar* is bound in with the last volume of the *Dictionary*). Another very important work arising from this upsurge of interest in the English dialects was A. J. Ellis's *On early English pronunciation, part V: The existing phonology of English dialects compared with that of West Saxon speech*, (1889).[15] In 1906, a Scandinavian dialectologist, J. Kjederqvist, published a little-known and highly technical monograph *The dialect of Pewsey (Wiltshire)*.

In 1939 appeared the English Place-Name Society's Wiltshire volume (PNW), edited by Gover, Mawer and Stenton. (The Wiltshire Archaeological & Natural History Society (WANHS) library contains an interleaved copy with much additional and valuable information supplied chiefly by T. R. Thomson.) Mention should be made too, of the Wiltshire Record Society's editions of important historical county documents, some of which include useful glossaries.[16]

As stated in the Preface, this study has been based mainly on the *Survey of English dialects* (SED). The SED was planned in 1946 to record traditional rural vernacular

5 *Edward Hungerford Goddard, a portrait in Devizes Museum.*

throughout England; of the 313 localities covered, nine were in Wiltshire: Ashton Keynes, Sutton Benger, Avebury, Burbage, Steeple Ashton, Netheravon, Sutton Veny, Fovant and Whiteparish. The Survey's all-important Questionnaire, specially biased towards farming people, was finalised in 1952 and contained some 1300 questions designed to elicit items of lexical (mostly), phonological, morp-

9

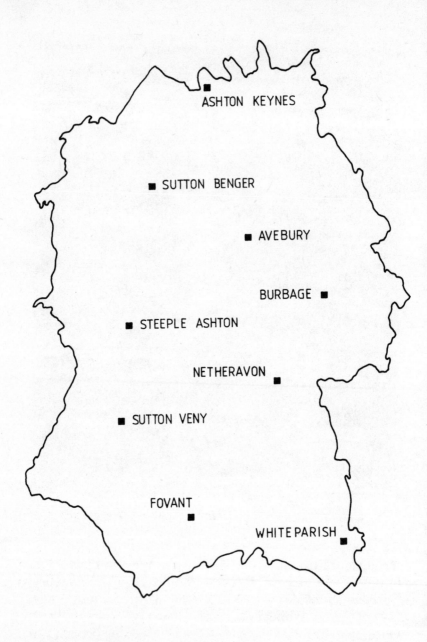

6 *The Wiltshire localities from the* Survey of English dialects.

THE FARMSTEAD

Show an aerial photograph of a farmstead and surrounding fields ☐.

1 ... these? **Fields.**
2 ... this? **Farmstead.**
3 ... this? **Farmyard.**
4 ... this? **Stackyard.**
  ... the various buildings?

If necessary, ask the relevant question below.

5 ... the place where you keep pigs? **Pigsty.**—April 1953, *the animals that go (i. grunting) replaced pigs.*

6 ... the place where you keep hens? **Hen-house.**—April 1953, *the birds that lay eggs for you replaced hens.*

7 ... the place where you keep pigeons? **Dove-cote.**—April 1953, *the birds that go (i. cooing) replaced pigeons.*

8 ... the place where you keep your cows? **Cow-house.**—April 1953, *the animals that give you milk replaced your cows.*

9 ... the yard in which cattle are kept, especially during the winter, for fattening, and for producing dung? **Straw-yard.**
  Verify the kind of cattle and the purpose.

10 ... the small enclosed piece of pasture near the farmhouse, the place where you might put a cow or a pony that's none too well? **Paddock.**

11 Rev. What's the **barn** for and where is it?

7 *Section of the* Survey of English dialects *questionnaire dealing with the farmstead. (N.B. Interview instructions:* ... = *"What do you call"; i = imitate. Revisions made to some questions in 1953 were to avoid bias towards eliciting the words paraphrased in the informant's answer.)*

hological and syntactical significance. The fieldwork was carried out by nine professionally trained fieldworkers between 1948 and 1961; *The Southern Counties* volume recording was carried out between 1952 and 1959. The responses to the Questionnaire, together with a substantial amount of "incidental material" were published in four volumes, each divided into three parts; *The Southern Counties* (Volume IV) which includes Wiltshire and the neighbouring counties, was published in 1967 and 1968. Two invaluable spin-offs from this mountain of research are Orton and Wright, *A word geography of England* (WGE) (1974), mapping 207 lexical items together with an analytical introduction, and the

Orton, Sanderson and Widdowson, *Linguistic atlas of England* (LAE) (1978), which provides 474 interpretative maps of the whole country, lexical (80), phonological (301), morphological (84), and syntactical (9).[17]

The most recent general book on the English dialects is Martyn Wakelin's excellent *English dialects: an introduction* (revised edition 1977), and our dependence on this work will be readily apparent to anyone familiar with it. Another excellent wide-ranging recent work, which includes discussion of the varieties of English spoken outside Britain, is John Wells's *Accents of the English* (1982). Somewhat difficult to get hold of, but otherwise the most recent and quite technical study of the South-West dialects, based on SED and EDD, is Fischer's *Dialects in the South-West of England, a lexical investigation* (1976), and the much more readable study by Norman Rogers, *Wessex dialect* (1979). An interesting side-light is thrown on the South-West lexicon by the material collected in a fascinating and recently published work edited by Widdowson, *A dictionary of Newfoundland English* (DNE) (1982).[18]

NOTES

1 Samuels, M., 1963. "Some applications of Middle English dialectology". *English Studies* 44:1–14.

2 Also of initial *s* to *z*, and probably of initial θ to ð and *sh* to *zh*, but early evidence of the first is usually, and of the second and third always, masked by Middle English spelling conventions.

3 For a detailed discussion of the modern situation (based on the *Survey of English dialects* (SED)), see Francis, W. N., Svartvik, J. and Rubin, G. M., 1969. "Computer-produced representation of dialectal variation: initial fricatives in southern British English." *International conference on computational linguistics* 54; and Wakelin, M. F., and Barry, M. V., 1968. "The voicing of initial fricative consonants in present-day dialectal English", pp. 47–64 in Ellis, S. *Studies in honour of Harold Orton on the occasion of his seventieth birthday* (Leeds Studies in English 2).

4 It may be of interest to note here, however, that the Southern dialects

of Middle English retained this initial voicing long enough to ensure that some Southern forms became accepted into the standard language, such are: *vane* (the spelling *fane* is found as late as the end of the eighteenth century); *vat* (the spelling *fat* survived into the eighteenth century); the dressmaker's *vent* (*fent* survives in dialect); and, perhaps most interestingly, *vixen* (as opposed to *fox*, with initial *f* sound. *Fixen* survived into the early eighteenth century; the *Oxford English dictionary's* (OED) first citation beginning with *v* is from Shakespeare's *A Midsummer Night's Dream* III.ii.324., of *c*.1595).

5 Gover, J. E. B., Mawer, A. and Stenton, F. M., 1939. *The place-names of Wiltshire* (PNW), 330.

6 Samuels, M., 1963. *op.cit.*; McIntosh, A. *et. al.*, 1986. *A linguistic atlas of late medieval English*.

7 ȝ, the letter known as "yogh", represents a modern *y* sound, so that the form written *yȝeve* was pronounced *i-yév*, i.e. as two syllables (or sometimes three, when the final *e* was given full syllabic status), the first syllable being written as *y* but pronounced like a modern short *i*.

8 Horstmann, C. (ed.) 1883. *S. Editha sive chronicon Vilodunense*; there are copies in the Wiltshire Archaeological and Natural History Society Library at Devizes, and the Headquarters Local Studies Library, Trowbridge.

9 Personal communication. This is one of the sources mapped in McIntosh, A. *et al.*, 1986. *op. cit.*

10 Anon. 1636. *The King and Qveenes Entertainement at Richmond*. This has been edited by Bang, W. and Brotanek, R. 1903. *Materialen zur Kunde des älteren englischen Dramas*. Volume 2. A copy is held in the Library of the Wiltshire Archaeological and Natural History Society at Devizes, as *Wiltshire Tract 74:1*.

11 John Aubrey (1626–1697) has been described as a "Wiltshire antiquary and collector of gossip and curious information" and this is reflected in his publications, the best known of which, *Brief lives*, is a collection of biographies, chiefly of seventeenth-century worthies. His *Natural history of Wiltshire* is a "strange collection of facts, fancies and recipes" more of topographical content than biological; the manuscripts which make up the work were written between 1656 and 1691 but they did not appear in print until 1847 when they were edited by John Britton for the Wiltshire Topographical Society.

12 John Yonge Akerman (1806–73) was a leading numismatist and antiquary of his day. He was secretary to the Society of Antiquaries and edited their journal, *Archaeologia*. He published many papers of his own, principally on numismatics,

13 Edward Hungerford Goddard (1854–1947) was born at Alderton, educated at Winchester and Oxford, and held curacies at South Hinksey,

Oxford and Hilmarton. In 1883 he took the living at Clyffe Pypard where he remained for 52 years before retiring to Devizes. For much of that time he ran the Wiltshire Archaeological and Natural History Society virtually single-handed, being General Secretary and Editor from 1890 to 1942 and Librarian from 1909 to 1942. He was a prolific writer on a wide range of subjects, being of the Victorian polymath tradition.

George Edward Dartnell (1852–1908) was educated at Marlborough and spent his professional life in banking. He had a deep knowledge of certain branches of English literature, in particular contemporary poetry and fiction. He was a prolific writer of short poems; from 1881–1903 thirty-six of his poems and translations of French and German poems were printed in the *Journal of education* and he won twenty-three prizes for them. Apart from his collaborative project with Goddard on *Wiltshire words*, he was a major contributor to the *English dialect dictionary*.

14 Three word-lists entitled "Contributions towards a Wiltshire glossary" were published in *WAM* 26 (1892): 84–171; 291–314; 27 (1893): 124–159, and subsequently appeared as a bound volume *Wiltshire words: A glossary of words used in the county of Wiltshire* which includes an Addenda not published in *WAM*. Two sets of further Addenda were published later: *WAM* 30 (1899): 233–270 and *WAM* 46 (1934): 478–519,

15 Nor should the stimulus of Prince Louis Bonaparte's work in the 1870s be forgotten, conveniently summarised in Fischer, A., 1976. *Dialects in the South-West of England, a lexical investigation*.

16 The Wiltshire Record Society was founded in 1937, as the Records Branch of the Wiltshire Archaeological and Natural History Society, to promote the publication of the documentary sources for the history of Wiltshire. Over forty volumes, presenting edited versions of primary source material, have now been published.

17 These details of SED's coverage, and of its allied publications, are summarised from Wakelin, M., 1977 (revised edition). *English dialects: an introduction*. Recent, as yet unpublished, Wiltshire dialect material has also been collected by the Centre for English Cultural Tradition and Language, University of Sheffield (Paul Smith, *personal communication*).

18 In recent years a number of other thorough general treatments of dialect have been published, including: Trudgill, P. and Hughes, A., 1979. *English accents and dialects: an introduction to social and regional varieties of British English*; Trudgill, P. and Chambers, J. K., 1980. *Dialectology*; and Francis, R., 1983. *Dialectology: an introduction*.

2
Phonology

INTRODUCTION

When we think of "dialect" we think first perhaps of local accent, and then of one or two strange words we have heard used locally and whose meaning we have had to inquire. Students of dialect refer to these two aspects of the subject as PHONOLOGY and LEXICON respectively, or, with regard to the distribution of dialect words, WORD GEOGRAPHY. The third aspect, that perhaps does not spring so readily to mind, is GRAMMAR, that is, for example, the use of *I be* where standard English would say *I am*.

Historical representations

Already, by introducing the term STANDARD ENGLISH (StE), we have begun to define what we understand a dialect to be: – we feel it to be, in some way, non-standard. (Earlier commentators often felt it to be – mistakenly – *sub*-standard: this sort of value-judgement has no place in the scientific study of language.) Already by Chaucer's day, the late fourteenth century (and occasionally, even earlier), it was recognised that people from different parts of England spoke in different ways, and already, in *The Reeve's Tale*, he gives us a parody of a dialect very "foreign" to his own variety of London English, which – in the nature of such broad comedy – we can tell is intended to be Northern, but is not to be more precisely located. In self-conscious literature thereafter, at

15

least into the nineteenth century, the use of "dialect" is almost always intended to be humorous: the sixteenth and seventeenth century playwrights give their rustics a "stage" dialect which is broadly Southern, often intended as South Western (SW), but at any rate clearly divergent from the Metropolitan norm established from the late fifteenth century.[1]

In Shakespeare's *King Lear*, for example, of *c.*1605, he gives the disguised "court character", Edgar, the additional disguise of rustic dialect (IV.vi.236–247), for example: "Chill not let go, zir, without vurther 'casion". This line serves well to illustrate some of the obvious features of this stage dialect; the voicing of initial *s* to *z* and of initial *f* to *v*, and the use of the (archaic) pronoun *ich*[2] (here contracted and elided with *will*). The same all-purpose rustic dialect is given to a Devonshireman in the play, *The London Prodigal*, performed by Shakespeare's company probably in the very year he was writing *King Lear*. In his *Bartholomew Fair* of 1614, Ben Jonson even records the voicing of initial *sh* to the sound heard in StE *measure* (i.e. like French *je*) in the word *shrink*, printed as *zhrink* in the text.[3]

Dialect Boundaries

Despite the title of this study, it must be emphasised from the outset that – while a language may be – no dialect is an island, and most of the features discussed below apply to the other South-Western dialects – it is really only the individual illustrations selected that are specifically Wiltshire.

The dialect spoken in Wiltshire is a member of the South-Western grouping of dialects whose eastern limit, as defined by analysis of SED material, we can take to be marked roughly by a line running from the city of Gloucester around the north-eastern Wiltshire county boundary and diagonally through Hampshire to the south coast at Portsmouth (there is, of course, nothing definite about any such boundary). Fischer[4] has drawn attention to the significant fact that

16

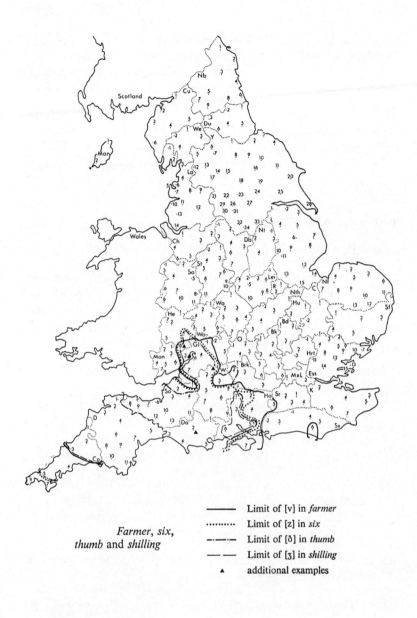

Farmer, six,
thumb and *shilling*

——— Limit of [v] in *farmer*
·········· Limit of [z] in *six*
—·—·— Limit of [ð] in *thumb*
— — Limit of [ʒ] in *shilling*
▲ additional examples

8 *The boundaries of the south-western dialect area as established by the voicing of initial fricatives recorded by SED in the 1950s. From M. Wakelin's* English dialects: an introduction, *1977.*

... all the major dialect boundaries in the South-West run parallel to ridges of hills and other elevations, to county boundaries, or to both. This congruence of linguistic boundaries with natural and ancient political ones is a clear indication of their stability and age.

The larger groupings of local dialects are established both internally, with regard to their constituent dialects, and externally, with regard to neighbouring groupings, by the plotting on the map of significant phonological features common to one area.

THE PHONOLOGY

Initial Consonants

Thus, perhaps the main phonological characteristic of the dialect of Wiltshire, and a feature it has in common with all the other SW dialects, is the voicing of certain initial consonants which remain unvoiced or voiceless in StE. Three of these we have already identified from "stage" dialect:

StE initial *f* sound appears as SW initial *v* sound as in *varmer*, *veasants*;

StE initial *s* sound appears as SW initial *z* sound as in *zat*, *zun*, *zinders*;

StE initial *sh* sound appears as SW initial *zh* sound (like *s* in StE measure or the sound of French *je*) as in *zhugar*.

The fourth sound concerns the two sounds that the letters *th* can represent in StE (the difference between which, of course, cannot be shown in conventionally printed texts), i.e. θ as in StE *thistle*, and $\eth$ as in StE *this*:

StE initial θ sound appears as SW initial $\eth$ sound as in $\eth atch$ (i.e. like StE *that*);

StE initial *thr* sound appears as SW initial *dr* sound as in *dree*, *drow*.

It should be noted, however, that these sound-changes may be more prevalent in one word than in another, especially in

18

the third case, where, for example, four of the nine localities recorded in SED gave the response *zhugar*, but only one *zhoulder* and one *zhilling*, and none, **zheep*.

This process of voicing has probably been going on since Old English times (though it is hidden by the spelling conventions), and corroborative evidence of the long-established nature of these changes is occasionally available by implication in the form of "secondary mutations", for example where the VOICELESS initial consonant has been voiced at some point in the past (as set out above), and then the resulting VOICED consonant has itself undergone a second change. The responses recorded by SED for *thistle* are revealing here: Ashton Keynes, in the extreme north of the county, has the standard or RECEIVED PRONUNCI-ATION (RP), *thistle*, while the rest of the county has voiced to *ðistle*, except Netheravon, where *distle* was recorded, a secondary change, which is otherwise only evidenced much further west in Devon, Cornwall and West Somerset (a different secondary change, to *vistle*, is evidenced in South Somerset and Dorset). The form recorded at Ashton Keynes shows that village to be on the edge of the South-West dialect area – to the immediate north-east in Oxfordshire, *thistle* was the unanimous response. Similarly with *thiller* (shaft horse), where Ashton Keynes shows the StE pronunciation, Burbage and Whiteparish have voiced to *ðiller*, Sutton Benger, Avebury, Steeple Ashton, Netheravon and Sutton Veny have made the secondary change to *diller(d)*, and Fovant, a different secondary change, to *viller*. With *fellies* (sections of wooden wheel rim), the north of the county has voiced to *vellies*, but the south of the county has seemingly "corrected" this form – as if it were a secondary rather than a primary mutation – "back" to *ðillies*. (Compare Fovant's *viller* next to Whiteparish's *ðiller*.) This voicing of initial FRICA-TIVE consonants is now, however, "sharply RECESS-IVE"[5]: Note that Mrs Roger's dialect, though her home in Oare near Pewsey is well inside the South Western voicing boundary as defined by SED (see map), shows *no* such voic-

19

ing of initial $\theta\rightarrow\delta$. This phonological boundary has clearly now receded further west (see Appendix 3).

Vowels

The consonant changes are perhaps the most obvious to the ear, but there are equally important vowel changes (especially DIPHTHONGISATION) that characterise the South-West dialects; in our county, these are almost exclusively found in South Wiltshire (SWi) and are mainly apparent before the sound *sh*.

StE *o* sound before *sh* can appear as SWi *oi* or *I* sound as in *woish*, *wIsh* (StE *wash*);

StE *e* sound before *sh* can appear as SWi *ai* or *I* sound as in *draishl*, *drIshl* (StE *threshold*), and *draish*, *drIsh* (StE *thresh*);

StE *a* sound before *sh* can also appear as SWi *I* sound as in *Ish*[6] (StE *ash*), and *SlIsher* (StE *"slasher"* i.e. hedging-bill).

(SED also records one hesitant example of *baig* for StE *bag*, i.e. before *g*; see also *laig* for StE *leg* in Appendix 3 (Putten up the Banns), late nineteenth century from Wilton; and *e* before *g* in Chapter 5). Because of the strong character of the South Western *r*, the sounds of *a* and *o* before *r* have, in some parts of the county at least, virtually merged, both being pronounced approximately like the *ar* of StE *ark*. This means, for example, that in the pairs *barn*: *born*; *card*: *cord*; *farm*: *form*; *hard*: *hoard*; *lard*: *lord*; *part*: *port*; and *park*: *pork*, both words may be pronounced identically.[7]

Semi-vowels

A third set of phonological changes affects the category of sounds known as SEMI-VOWELS, and here we are mainly concerned with the sounds represented in spelling by the letters *w* and *y*; these sounds are sometimes lost where they exist in StE, and sometimes added where they do not.

StE initial *w* sound before *u* (the *u* sound in StE *bush*) is lost in SW as in *ool*, *oman*, *ooden*;

StE initial *y* sound is often lost in SW most notably in the SED material in *east* (StE *yeast* from six of the nine localities; there is one example of *'is* for StE *yes*, and three of *'isterday*);

As an additional sound or GLIDE, SW dialects often

1. add *w* (a) Initially to a word beginning with an *oa* sound in StE, as in SW *wold*, *wook* and *woom* (where "*oo*" has the *u* sound in StE *bush*) or *wuck* and *wum*, for StE *old*, *oak* and *home*.[8] The last, of course, suggests that the initial *h* was dropped first, and the word was then treated as if it began with a vowel).

   (b) Between an initial consonant sound and a following *oa* or *oi* (or occasionally, *ai*) sound as in *twoad*, *stwonewall*, *bwoys* (heard throughout the county), *bwoiling* (except Ashton Keynes), and *pwoisinous* (except the extreme south of the county).

2. add *y* (a) Initially to a word beginning with a vowel, as in *year* (StE *ear*, heard throughout the county; so too for StE *hear*, compare remark concerning *woom*, *wum* above), *yeariwigs*, *yarm*, *yelm*, *yaporn* (StE *apron*), *yiccups* and *yerrins* (StE *herrings*. For these last two words, compare remark concerning *woom*, *wum* above).

   (b) (occasionally) Between an initial consonant and a following vowel sound, as in *byeans* and *gyate*.

Other Changes Involving the Sounds Represented by the Letters *H* and *R*

In English dialects generally, initial *h* is dropped; in four small areas of the country, however, one of which includes the southern part of our county together with Somerset and North Dorset, initial *h* is retained. Where it *is* dropped, this can lead to such curiosities as *an orse*. D&G comment: "Formerly it was the rarest thing in the world to hear a true Wiltshire rustic make such a slip, though the townsfolk were by no means blameless in this respect..." and, "It was virtually unknown sixty or seventy years ago [i.e. *c*.1820–1830], and even so late as thirty years back [i.e. *c*.1860] was still unusual in our villages. But the plague is fast spreading..."[9] Disregarding the judgmental tone, it appears that the position, for South Wiltshire, at least, as recorded in SED *c*.1960, would have pleased Mr. Dartnell and Canon Goddard, and is certainly excellent testimony to the conservatism of Wiltshire dialect, which has thus resisted a change effected in almost the whole of the country. Speaking of South-West Wiltshire *c*.1870, the Rev. G. Hill wrote to them that "the putting [of *h*] where it ought not to be did not I think exist. I find now that the *h* is ... occasionally added ..." We have noted two examples of such HYPERCORRECTION from the SED material: a *howl* (in the idiom, daft as a *howl*, from Sutton Benger), and *a hapril fool* (from Whiteparish).

John Wells in his *Accents of the English* (1982) writes: "The preservation of historical *r* in all environments is the best known phonetic characteristic of the West of England. Full RHOTICITY is to be observed in any kind of broad Western accent..."[10] In RP, an *r* written at the end of a word is not normally pronounced; thus, in RP, *beer, better, sister*, etc. end in a vowel sound. Similarly, *r* between a vowel and a consonant is not normally heard either; thus, in RP, *barn, girl, pork, short*, etc., end in a lengthened vowel sound followed by the consonant in question. The South Western *r*, however, known technically as RETROFLEX, *is* heard in all these words with "historical" *r*, and even at the end of words that never had "historical" *r*, e.g. *china, banana*, etc. – all are pronounced in the dialect with an audible final *r* sound. This "hyper-rhoticity" (as it is called) is even found in words where RP has a final unstressed *oa* sound, e.g. *window*, *yellow*, etc., which, in the South-Western counties end in the neutral vowel[11] followed by the *r* sound. (And this ending is thus pronounced in the dialect exactly like the ending of the *better*, *sister* type.)

The quality of the *r* sound in the South-West is also such that it sometimes produces METATHESIS, that is, a swopping round of sounds so that, for example, *brush* becomes *bursh* (recorded from Avebury and from Steeple Ashton); *curdle* becomes *criddle* (from Steeple Ashton. The *Oxford English dictionary* (OED) notes *cruddle(d)* in StE from *c.*1600; it occurs, for example, in the 1611 *Authorised Version* of the *Bible*, at Job X.10. In fact, present-day *curd*, from which *curdle* derives, is itself a metathesised form of original *crudde*, so perhaps we should rather say that StE *curdle* is the metathesised form, and that dialect preserves the earlier form); *gurt* (unanimous for *great*) and *purdy* i.e. *pretty* (only once, from Whiteparish, but *purt'* is recorded from Burbage used adverbially in *purt' near a poun'*). The informant from Steeple Ashton provided most of the examples we have noted in SED, and it should be observed that such metathesis is a common feature of this particular informant's speech, e.g. *burge* (StE *bridge*), and the initial metathesis *urnse*, in *urnse the clothes out*. When metathesis occurs initially, it is usually ASPIRATED as well, that is, an *h* sound is added to the beginning of the word, e.g. *hurp* for StE *rip* (in *hurp'ook* i.e. *rip-hook*, itself a SW dialect variant of StE *reap-hook* i.e. sickle, recorded in SED under *bill-hook*), *hurd* for StE *red*, and *hurst* for StE *wrist* (all from Steeple Ashton). It is perhaps also worth noticing that the full *l* sound is sometimes preserved in South-Western dialects, i.e. it is sounded in words like *palm* and *calm*, which RP pronounces simply as a lengthened *a*, followed by *m* – this accounts too, for one local pronunciation of *Calne*, which in RP is identical with *Khan*.[12]

NOTES

1 See Chapter 1.
2 An analysis of the mixed nature of Edgar's dialect may be found in Blake, N. F. 1976. "Born in Kent", *Lore and language* 2(5): 5–9.
3 If this is not merely a mechanical transposition of initial *z* for every initial *s*.
4 Fischer, A. 1976. *op. cit.* 360.
5 For data see Francis, W. N., Svartvik, J. and Rubin, G. M. 1969. *op. cit.*; Wakelin, M. F. and Barry, M. V. 1968. *op. cit.*; and Wells, J. 1982. *Accents of the English*. 343. *t* is also found voiced to *d* medially, for example, in *butter*, pronounced *budder*, especially in the South-West (Wells, 344), and *p* to *b*, *k* to *g*, *ch* to *j*. It is, however, frequently still heard in the dialect of Newfoundland, which contains many South-Western features (see DNE's remarks under *var*).
6 Note that Dartnell and Goddard in their 1934 Addenda record *aishen*, i.e. made of ash wood, but it is not clear how this is to be interpreted phonologically.
7 Wells, J. 1982. *op. cit.* 347 and LAE maps Ph48 and Ph19.
8 It is of interest to note here that StE has adopted from SW dialect the *w* glide in its pronunciation of *one* i.e. *wun*.
9 Extracts quoted from entry under *H* and Introduction p. xvii, respectively.
10 Wells, J. 1982. *op. cit.* 341
11 Represented in the phonetic alphabet by the symbol *ə*, the sound of the *a* at the end of the word *comma*, for example.
12 Wells, J. 1982. *op cit.* 346. But note the spelling *Caan* in Appendix 3 (The Cannings Vawk); the authors have also recorded *cown* in the Avebury district.

3

Grammar and Syntax

GRAMMAR

Under this heading we shall deal with the ways in which Wiltshire dialect usage differs from that of the standard language in its treatment of the parts of speech.

Nouns

PLURALS

SED records several double plurals for Wiltshire, including *wantses* (StE *moles*), strictly a possessive plural, as received in the compound *wantses-run* (StE? *mole-track*) from Sutton Benger; more widespread is *belluziz* (for StE *(pair of) bellows*) from six of the nine localities, and *hameziz, ameziz* or *yameziz* (for StE *hames*: (curved pieces which form or are attached to the collar of a draught-horse and to which the traces are fixed), from seven of the localities.

Of the irregular plurals, *tooths* was recorded once only from Sutton Veny. StE *chickens* is in fact a double plural, *-en* being an old plural ending (compare *oxen*); the "correct" plural, *chicken*, was found throughout Wiltshire. D&G under *Plurals* note that [*c*.1890] "The old termination in *en* is still much used, as *Housen, Hipsen*, etc.," but none were recorded by SED. D&G also note that nouns ending in *-st* frequently make their plurals by adding an extra syllable *-iz*; see SED under *gate-posts* (six localities have the extra syllable. Note too, *getpwostiz* from Burbage with the additional intrusive *w* glide-vowel).

25

Dialect also occasionally makes count-nouns (i.e. nouns capable of having a plural) out of nouns that are mass-nouns in the standard language, for example, *stubbles*.

COMPOUNDING

There are differences too, in the formation of compounds: compare *vowulzouse* from three of the localities as opposed to *vowulouse* (StE *hen-house*), i.e. showing a possessive construction.

Pronouns

PERSONAL

We have seen that one of the features felt to mark out the South-Western dialects was its retention of the archaic form of the first person singular pronoun, *ich* for StE *I*. D&G do not mention this form in their late nineteenth-century glossary, nor does it appear in any of the earlier nineteenth-century sources, and it probably went out of use generally in the eighteenth century. It is all the more remarkable, then, that as late as 1952, *ich* was recorded by an SED field-worker near Montacute in Somerset, a mere 30 or so miles from the Wiltshire border.[1]

In dialect, *I* is frequently found where the standard language would have *me*, for example, *"gi'out 'n' let I take over"*, and *"gi' 't back to I"* and *"will you come wi' I?"* Similarly with the first person plural, where the standard language would use the grammatically incorrect form, *us*, dialect will use *we*: "It's only we." *Us* for StE *me* is a widespread English colloquialism, compare from Whiteparish, *"cu's'tell us the time?"* (i.e. *couldst* etc.). Dialect also retains the second person singular, *thou*, and *thee*, only used archaically in modern English (for example in the *Lord's Prayer*), as part of its everyday usage; again both can be used ungrammatically: *"please(d) t'zee thou"*; though the opposite, *thee* for *thou*, is much commoner, for example, *"'owbis' thee?"*, and "*'as' thee got the toothyache?*". *He* and *him* may similarly change roles – a feature limited to South-Western dialect – but their situation is complicated by the interesting survival in our area of a third form, *'n*, the original Old English accusative or object case of the third person singular masculine, which the standard language replaced with the dative case (compare modern German, where the original state of affairs in Old English still survives: accusative *ihn*, dative *ihm*). For example, it is the almost unanimous SED response for StE *ask him*, which becomes *asks 'n* [*sic*]. Just as with the pronouns already considered, however, it is also used occasionally ungrammatically as the subject of the verb, for example, *ent 'n?* from Avebury for StE *isn't he?* *'n* is also used for StE *it* in the object case, compare *(h)ide'n* (of a bone). In the sentence "*you'll zee 'n comin' back wi' 'n*" from Whiteparish, *'n* is used for both *him* and *it*. It should be noted that cases of apparent *her* for *he*, for example, *do 'er?* (*does he?*), and *idn' 'er?* (*isn't he?*) both from Fovant, are not what they seem, being, in fact, an unstressed form of *he* with normal South-West *r*-COLOURING. As with *he* and *him*, so with the feminine pronoun; *'er* (i.e. StE *her*) is usual for StE *she* in the South-West (so too in the Central and South-West Midlands), and *she* may similarly appear for *her*, as in *brought she up*, from Sutton Veny.

As for the third person plural pronoun, in an unemphatic context, *'m* is used where the standard language has *they*, for example, *(b)ent 'm?* for *aren't they?* This may also not be what it appears, a clipped form of StE *them*, but an interesting survival of ME *hem* (which is *not* the origin of StE *them*). It is possible that the form, *the'*, at least when used accusatively, recorded consistently from Steeple Ashton, may represent a transitional form intermediate between *'m* and *they*, perhaps under the influence of StE *them*.

There is evidently a general rule applying to the apparently haphazard way in which a subject form of a pronoun may change places with its object form, and that is determined by its context in the sentence; object for subject form

27

only occurs in an unemphatic situation, and similarly the subject form is only used for the object in an emphatic context.

POSSESSIVE

Archaic *thy* (pronounced *thi*) is naturally as widespread as its second person singular personal forms, compare: *"go 'n' wipe thi mouth"*, *"I knowed thi voice"*, and *"pokin' thi tongue out"*. The use of *its* is sometimes avoided in dialect, and *his* is sometimes used instead (in fact, the archaic neuter possessive pronoun, preserved down to the seventeenth century in StE, compare, from the 1611 *Authorised Version* of the *Bible*: "The tent, and all his furniture . . . his boards, his barres, and his pillars, and his sockets" (Exodus XXXIX.33. cit. OED *his* 3c) or else a PERIPHRASTIC (i.e. a roundabout way of avoiding *its*) construction such as *of 'n*. Along with *thy*, of course, *thine* is also in general use, and the influence of this form and of *mine* has generalised an *-n* ending onto the rest of this set of pronouns, i.e. *hisn*, *hern*, *ourn*, *yourn*, *theirn* – a feature of English dialects in general (except Northern).

REFLEXIVE

Thyself is also current. *Hisself* appears for StE *himself*, and *theirzelf* or *theirzelves* for StE *themselves*. Occasionally the singular personal pronoun will take the place of the reflexive *-self* form, for example, from Sutton Veny, *wash me*, for StE *wash myself*. Sometimes dialect uses a reflexive construction (though not necessarily the *-self* form) where StE would not, for example, from Whiteparish, *"zit thee down there"*.

DEMONSTRATIVE

There is some confusion over the use of *this*, *that*, *thick*, and *thuck* (the two last being pronounced with the same *th* sound as StE *this* and *that*, and being dialect survivals of ME *thilke*). In short, *thick* can mean either *this* or *that*, but *thuck*, a North Wiltshire (NWi) form only (recorded in SED from Ashton Keynes and Sutton Benger), can only mean *that*; con-

28

sequently, the normal constrastive pair may be *this* and *that* as in StE (from Ashton Keynes); *thick* and *thuck* (from Sutton Benger); *thick* and *that* (from Avebury, Sutton Veny, Fovant and Whiteparish); or even, from Netheravon, *these*[2] and *thick*. For StE *these*, a curious form, *theesm*, was recorded from Burbage and Netheravon; it is not impossible that this is a survival of the OE dative plural, *thisum* (compare the fact that both StE *them*, and dialect *'m* possibly derive from dative plurals). D&G, under *Pronouns*, give *thesen* as an occasional SWi variant (not recorded by SED), so the explanation might rather be that *theesm* is for *theesn*, i.e. *these*+*'ns* (=*ones*). Wakelin[3] wonders whether it might not be a blend of *these* + *them*, or perhaps we might suggest, *these* + *'m*. (*theem* from Fovant for *these*, is probably a shortened form of *theesm*, and is most unlikely to be StE *them* which is not found in Wiltshire dialect – see remarks at *'m* above.)

DISJUNCTIVE

There is a further type of pronoun usage which is not found in StE, and is to be distinguished from the (rude) form of address available to StE. There can be no question of impoliteness in the responses to SED (asking someone the time), for example: *"tell us the toim you"*, *"what time is it you?"* and *"wha's the time you?"*; nor in those to *What direction is the wind?*, for example: *"which way's the wind you?"* and *"where's the wind got to you?"* Similarly for StE *How are you?* note *"'ow bis' thee getn on you?"* and the invitation, *"come (on) in you"*.

RELATIVE

The woman that lived in this house is nowadays quite acceptable as StE, only the pedantic would insist on *who*, and this usage is also found in dialect, but so too, are *what* and *as* (the latter, StE as late as Shakespeare's day, compare *Romeo & Juliet* II.i.36., "that kind of fruit As maids call medlars", and for long after). SED records the following: *He is the man*

29

"what d' look after the cows"; *"the pig'ales* [i.e. *haws*] *what comes off o' the may"*; *"we got one what we keep ourn in"*; *"a thing as isn't done today"*; *"a varmer as 'adn't 'ad no sheep"*; *"our rent-man as comes"*. Dialect can also omit the relative where StE cannot, for example: *He* *"is the man look after the cows"*; *"there idn't many does it"*; *"there's one look in-toed"* [for *hen-toed*, i.e. *pigeon-toed*].

Adjectives

TYPES OF FORMATION

In StE many adjectives with the meaning "consisting or made of – " were formed by the addition of the suffix *-en* to a noun in the Middle English period, for example, StE *wooll-en, wood-en*. It has long been a well-known feature of South-West dialect to extend this principle to almost any material. For Wiltshire, SED records *a tharnen hedge* (i.e. *of thorn*) from Fovant (compare the place-name, Birch*en* Coppice, near Downton); *stonenlather* (for *stone-ladder*, i.e. *stone stile*) from Sutton Benger; *eldernberries* also from Sutton Benger, may not be another example, for the tree itself is called *aldern* at Ashton Keynes, and the OE form also had final *-rn*, and OED records such a form (under *elder*) as late as 1608, and ours may simply be a dialect survival of this. (But note the StE tree names, asp*en* and lind*en*, which *were* formed adjectivally from the names of their woods.) Under *En* (2), D&G record many more examples of this formation, but with only two certain instances from SED for Wiltshire, it seems that, like the plural suffix *-en*, this too is moribund, if not – in 1987 – extinct altogether. (It is, however, preserved in Newfoundland English; in their introduction to DNE, the editors give as "one of the principal grammatical features of various folk-speech types to be found in N.Labrador: 2. Adjectives derived from names of materials end in *-en: tinnen cup, glassen pole.*")[4]

Since the late Middle English period, certain existing adjectives have been extended by means of a *-y* termination, with the object of making them look "more adjectival", for example, *hugy* from *huge*. The majority of such "double" adjectives arose in the sixteenth and seventeenth centuries, for example, *chilly* from *chill*, *lanky* from *lank*, *hoary* from *hoar*, etc. In contemporary colloquial English, the same process may be seen at work in the colour adjectives in particular, for example, *yellowy* from *yellow*, *greeny* from *green*, etc. where the *-y* ending perhaps has a force similar to *-ish*, i.e. *rather*. Though not recorded from Wiltshire in SED's responses for *round*, Mr Norman Rogers attests the existence of *roundy* in our dialect. SED does, however, record one example of this phenomenon in *brittly* from *brittle* from informants in Sutton Benger and Fovant.[5]

COMPARISONS
Dialect generally is inclined to make comparatives with the *-er* termination where StE would use *more* + the adjective, for example, dialect *usefuller*, StE *more useful*, and also to make double comparatives, for example, *more safer*; similarly with superlative formations, for example, dialect *usefullest* and *most usefullest*, StE *most useful*. Irregular adjectives, for example, the StE series, *bad*, *worse*, *worst*, are particularly prone to dialect variants, for example, from Burbage and Sutton Veny, *worser*, in " '*tis worser still*".

Conjunctions

Also a general English dialect usage is the archaic *for to* for StE *to* in the sense *in order to*, often shortened simply to *for*, or omitted altogether, for example, *went see* from Avebury, for StE *went to see*.

Prepositions

Equally widespread is the use of *off* followed by *of*; the "*pig'ales what comes off o' the may*"; while *of*, especially

31

when followed by a vowel, often becomes *on*, compare *out on it*.

Verbs

PRESENT TENSE

One characteristic of South-Western dialect is a third person singular without the StE *-s* ending; this feature is especially noticeable in forms recorded from Sutton Benger: *"she wear the breeches"*, and *"stop, it 'urt"*: and – a nice piece of dialect exhibiting several of the features we have already noted above – *"no-one as I know on keep they"*. Conversely, especially after a plural noun, the verb, instead of having no ending as in StE, often has an *-s* ending (especially common from Netheravon in the SED responses), for example, *"'arses whickers"*, *"cows maws"*, *"sheep baas"*, *"cats mews"*; *"they sheep knows it"*; *"burglars steals 'm"*; *"they bides 'ome"*; *"they goes t' church"*. This is quite common with the irregular verb *be*, i.e. dialect *is, was* for StE *are, were*: *"my hands is spreathed"* (i.e. *chapped*); *"they cows was right"*; *"those eggs is ready to pop"* (i.e. *hatch*); *"these cheddies is a bit fresh"* (i.e. *these potatoes need a little salt*); *"and the ol' diddikies is up Black Lane"* (i.e. *gipsies*). In some cases, the third person singular ending, *-s*, as well as being extended to the third person plural as here, has been extended to other persons; compare *"I keeps"* from Ashton Keynes, and *"off you goes"* from Avebury and Sutton Veny.

INFINITIVE

In Old English many infinitives (the form of the verb that, for example, follows an auxiliary verb, such as *can*) ended in the disyllable, *-ian*; although the *-an* had disappeared, SW dialect long preserved the *-i-*, compare D&G under *Y*: "The free infinitive in *-y* was formerly much used, but is now dying out. It was used in a general question, as '*Can you mowy?*' " That was *c*.1890. It is to be feared it is now well and truly dead, in Wiltshire at least. SED did, however, find an example in Devon: *"there idn' many can sheary now"*.[6]

PARTICIPLES

Both the present participle (in *-ing*), and the past participle (mostly in *-ed*), are often prefaced in dialect by *a-*, deriving from two different sources in OE. (The ME form of the past participle prefix, *y-* or *i-*, is occasionally found in modern English in such deliberate archaisms as *yclept*, meaning *called*.) The present participle in *a-* is common throughout central England as far south as Wiltshire: D&G could say in 1893, "The prefix *a* is always used with the present participle, as *a-gwain'*, *going*, *a-zettin' up*, *sitting up*". Compare SED's *a-gwoin'* and *a-gwain'* from Ashton Keynes and Fovant; *"what's that child a-doin' there?"* from Steeple Ashton and Netheravon; and *a-comin'* and *a-wanin' away* also from Ashton Keynes.

The past participle in *a-* is, however, mainly a South-Western feature. SED records for Wiltshire: *a-done* from all except two northern localities; *a-zeed* (StE *seen*) from Steeple Ashton; *a-broke* (StE *broken*) from Fovant; and *a-drunked* from Steeple Ashton, and *a-drinked* from Netheravon and Fovant (StE *drunk*).

PAST TENSE AND IRREGULAR PAST PARTICIPLES

The so-called STRONG verbs of StE, i.e. those which make their past tenses by changing the stem vowel, for example, *I swim. I swam. I have swum*, are often given the WEAK past ending, *-ed*, in dialect; for Wiltshire, SED records the following: *knowed*, *growed*, *zeed* and *catched*, for StE *knew*, *grew*, *saw* and *caught*; less universal examples are: *creeped*, *gived*, *speaked*, and *stealed*, for StE *crept* (from Ashton Keynes and Steeple Ashton), *gave* (from Ashton Keynes, Netheravon and Fovant), *spoke* (from Whiteparish), and *stole* (from Netheravon). In some cases weak endings are added to the "correct" past tense form: for example, *stoled* (from Sutton Benger and Whiteparish), and *layed* (from all localities) for StE *stole*, and *lay* (past tense of *lie*, though this latter error is a common enough confusion amongst StE speakers, due to the contextually similar verb *lay*, past tense *laid*).

Similarly, the weak ending is given to the past participles of strong verbs, notably *gived* and *stoled*, for StE *given* (the almost unanimous response), and *stolen* (from Sutton Benger and Whiteparish). A weak ending may even be added to a "correct" strong past participle, as in the case of *founded* and *(a)-drunked*, for StE *found* (from Sutton Veny) and *drunk* (from Sutton Benger and Steeple Ashton). The past tense of strong verbs is frequently extended to the past participle in dialect, for example: *broke*, *took*, and *drank*, for StE *broken* (unanimous), *taken* (unanimous), and *drunk* (from Sutton Benger), and even *went* for StE *gone* (from Whiteparish and Fovant). The reverse situation is found with the StE past participle form *begun*, used for the dialect past tense (StE *began*) at Steeple Ashton and Fovant, and *zeen* for StE *saw* from Avebury, Netheravon and Whiteparish. The overall tendency in the dialect participles of strong verbs is towards a reduction of the number of different forms, compare the one-form StE verbs such as *cut* and *put* (i.e. *I cut. I cut. I have cut.* etc.). The best example is *eat*, where seven of the nine localities show the same form, be it *eat* or *ate*, for all three different parts of the StE verb *eat. ate. eaten*. With *come* for StE *came*, which in StE has only two different parts, i.e. *come. came. come.*, the dialect has simplified the verb in the same way as it has, *eat*. This process seems to be especially prevalent at Netheravon, which replaces StE *it began*, and *I . . . saw*, with the present tense forms, *it begin* (note the endingless form as discussed above), and *I . . . zee*. Another example from Steeple Ashton, *I . . . ride*, for *I . . . rode*, perhaps indicates that this is a central Wiltshire phenomenon.

THE VERB "BE"

The verb, *be*, is a special case. The same tendency towards

34

one-form simplification, however, can again be discerned: by pooling the information from SED, we can see that at Avebury and Sutton Veny, instead of the three different StE present tense forms, *am. is. are.*, there is only the one form, *be.* (excluding, of course, the second person singular *thee bis(t)*, in general use, which StE no longer has). Thus, a typical, partial, paradigm for the present tense would run: *I be. thee bis(t). her (i)s. we be. they be.* Similarly, the past tense, StE *I was. she was. we were. they were.*, has been simplified to *was* throughout, at Ashton Keynes, and *were* throughout, at Steeple Ashton, Sutton Veny, Fovant and Whiteparish. With the past subjunctive after *if*, i.e. careful StE *if I/she/we were*, Steeple Ashton, Netheravon and Fovant conformed to StE usage here and used *were* throughout; Ashton Keynes, Sutton Benger, Avebury, Sutton Veny and Whiteparish on the other hand, dispensed with this historically correct subjunctive form altogether, and used *was* throughout, but significantly, Sutton Veny and Whiteparish do preserve the distinction of a different mood, for as we have just seen, these localities do not use *was* as their simple past tense form.

SED records *they'm* for StE *they are* from Whiteparish; what follows is an attempt to explain how this curious form may have arisen. The first person singular in Whiteparish is *I be*, as it is throughout Wiltshire, but was probably *I am* earlier (as evidenced in the Wiltshire dialect antimasque of 1636, line 185, *cham*, i.e. a contraction of *ich am*, Modern English *I am*), and *I'm, We (a)m*, and *they (a)m* are recorded from bordering localities in neighbouring counties; it is possible, therefore, that the *(a)m* form has merely been displaced from the first person singular to the third person plural, rather than been replaced altogether. *Art they?*, an alternative to the usual *be they?*, from Steeple Ashton, shows confusion with the (archaic) second person singular form *art thee?* recorded from that locality only (but see next paragraph), under the influence of StE *are they?*[7]

35

SYNTAX

Syntax is concerned with the way a phrase or sentence may be put together; naturally, this includes grammar, but it is also a matter of options – two alternative ways of saying something may both be correct, and yet one is preferred. Dialect, for example, occasionally shows a preference for the older simple form of the verb, over its modern StE expanded form, for example, Wakelin giving a sentence from Avebury recorded in unpublished SED material: *"Don't rain now, do it?"*, whose StE equivalent would use the expanded form, *"(It) isn't raining now, is it?"* Conversely, a characteristic of South-Western dialect is the use of the PERIPHRASTIC construction with *do* in simple positive statements, in place of the StE simple present tense. StE does, of course, use this construction with *do*, but only in certain contexts – interrogative, negative, and emphatic statements, for example, *Did he say that?*, *don't say that.*, and *He did (not) say that.* (and, indeed, at the beginning of this sentence!). Dialect distributes this usage differently, compare: *We ordinary people buy the things we need*, *"but burglars do steal"*, from Ashton Keynes, Steeple Ashton and Fovant, and, also from Fovant, *"some people do double-spid it"* (i.e. dig it down two spade-depths).

Dialect also distributes the definite and indefinite articles differently from StE, for example, StE *have you got toothache?* with no definite article, in dialect becomes, *"'s' thee go' the toothyache?"*, *"'s' thee got the jaws-ache?"*, etc. The StE response to the question, *About how many calves does a cow have?* might be *"about ten"*, but dialect adds the indefinite article to its response, for example, *"'boud a nine 'r ten"*, *"'boud a vower 'r vive"*, *"'b' a zix"*, etc.

NOTES

1 Wakelin, M. F. 1977. *op. cit.* 165 note 6.
2 Or does the International Phonetic Alphabet notation in SED imply, rather, *this?*

3 Wakelin, M. F. 1977. *op. cit.* 116. Dr. Wakelin, *pers. comm.*, now feels rather dubious about this explanation.
4 Dr. Wakelin has drawn our attention to a discussion of this point in Phillips's *West-Country words and ways.*
5 See also, D&G under *Y.*
6 Again, Dr. Wakelin has drawn our attention to a discussion of this point in Phillips's *West Country words and ways.*
7 Several other archaic second person singular forms of verbs are preserved sporadically in Wiltshire dialect (apart from *bis(t)*, that is, which we have already noticed above): the negative of *art thee?*, i.e. *artn' thee?*, from Netheravon; *weren' 'ee* from Sutton Benger, may represent the archaic and "correct" form (i.e. *weren't thou*) of the later *wast thee?* (*wersn'(t)* from southern localities, seems to imply a new unhistorical formation, **wer(e)st)*; *dos(t)* is common (for example, in the formation of periphrastic tenses – see following section); *'as'* (i.e. *hast*) and *cou's,* (i.e. *couldst*), are both found, for example, in "*'as' got the time on thee?*" and "*cou's' tell us the time?*"; (*durs'n* i.e. *durst not,* from *dare*) is recorded from Ashton Keynes and Sutton Benger. See further: OED under *be* A.6.

4

The General Lexicon

ORIGINS

The vocabulary or LEXICON of dialect is often the aspect of which we are most aware, the curious words whose meaning we have to inquire – some of them are as ephemeral as many of the colloquialisms in StE, some have an "old-fashioned" air about them, that, in fact, points to the great antiquity of others not immediately comprehensible to speakers of StE.

Time and time again, this archaism of dialect – or perhaps we should rather say, its extreme conservatism, which resists the introduction of new words – can be shown, most clearly in pairs of words one of which was formerly current in the standard language throughout England, but is now restricted to Wiltshire or South-Western dialect, while the other is now the normal StE word.

Dialect Retention of the Native Lexicon

Often the standard language has replaced the native word which dialect retains, with a foreign import. To take a simple example: if someone asked the name of "the animal that throws up small mounds of earth in the fields", the standard reply would be *mole*, but a native Wiltshireman would almost certainly reply, *want* or *waunt*, a word of venerable antiquity, being found already in an Old English glossary of the early eighth century, whereas the word, *mole*, is not recorded in English before *c*.1400. This is a case where dialect has preserved the original native word, which the standard

39

language has forgotten, replacing it with a word of LOW GERMAN (LG) origin.

Sometimes, both words in such a pair are equally familiar to speakers of StE, who may or may not be aware of a slight difference in usage or nuance; most speakers of StE would probably not be able to choose between *adder* and *viper* (or to justify their choice) as their response to the question, "What do you call the small poisonous snake we sometimes find in the country?" but dialect hardly ever uses the latter word, introduced from French in the early sixteenth century and first found in Tindale's *Bible* translation of 1526; it is the native word, *adder*, from OE *næd(d)re* that is used.[1] The word which StE uses to name the bristles of barley, *awns*, first recorded in the thirteenth century is ultimately derived from OLD NORSE (ON), and is also found in dialect, significantly distributed throughout the regions most thickly settled by the Danes; the South of England, including Wiltshire, which escaped Scandinavian settlement, uses the word, *ails*, from OE *egel*. A word more familiar to StE speakers is (hay) *stack*, also of Scandinavian origin (though not independently attested in English until the thirteenth century, ultimately from ON *stakkr*); the South-Western and South-West Midlands dialects preserve OE *hrēac*, i.e. *rick*. The responses to the SED question, "What do you call the white stuff that comes out of a festering wound?" to which the standard reply would be, *pus*, occasioned the unanimous response *matter*, in Wiltshire as it did, indeed, from the dialects as a whole; once again, this is the "older" word (though itself an import, probably via French), being found in this sense from *c*.1400, whereas *pus* is not found until 1541, a "learned" Latin word belonging to the technical language of medical treatises. Similarly, StE *vomit*, seems to have been a technical translator's word, and is not found until the fifteenth century,[2] while dialect retains the native verb, *spew*, formerly in standard use, of native Old English stock.

Similar cases concerning "newer" words of foreign origin replacing "older" words of native, Germanic stock could be

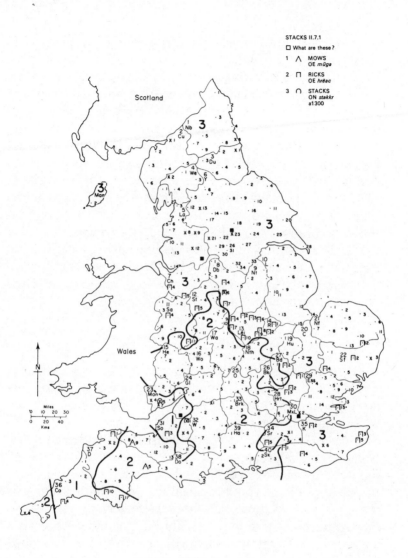

9 *Map showing the distribution of words for* (hay)stack *as recorded in SED (after WGE). Wiltshire is firmly within the* rick *area showing the preservation of the native OE word, as is to be expected in an area not settled by the Norsemen (i.e. the* stack *area).*

41

multiplied (though they are rarely found in general as opposed to local, dialect use), compare, for example, the word for what a hen rests on at night, StE *perch*, the response given throughout Wiltshire, except at Steeple Ashton, where the informant labelled this word as "modern", himself preferring, *roost*. He was right! *perch* is the more "modern" word, being first found in Chaucer's late fourteenth century *Canterbury Tales*, whereas *roost* belongs to the vocabulary of Old English: similarly the pairs, *brush* v. *broom*; and *beak* v. *bill*. The pair, dialect *afeared*, StE *afraid*, which might at first seem to be possible variants, are not; Chaucer recognises this in his phrase "this wif was nat afered ne afrayed" – again the dialect word is the older, going back to native Old English stock, while the now StE *afraid* is in origin a probable thirteenth century import from France, the past participle of the verb, *affray*, to frighten.

Variants within the Native Lexicon

VARIANT FORMS OF THE SAME WORD

There are several words, however, where dialect uses a different form from StE, though both are, in fact, merely variants of the same word (or may even reflect dialect differences reaching back to Old English), and there can be no question of the greater antiquity of either, it is a matter of different distributions, dialect having adopted one form, and the ancestor of StE (broadly speaking, the Middle English of the Central Midlands), another. Two such words, in use throughout Wiltshire and the Southern counties generally, are *emmet*, StE *ant*, and *evet*, StE *newt*. The first pair both derive from OE *ǣmete*, the second pair both from OE *efeta*. StE *newt* is an instance of a phenomenon known as MET-ANALYSIS or, more transparently, as FALSE DIVISION: at some point (probably in the fourteenth century) the combination with the indefinite article, i.e. "*an ewt*", was wrongly analysed as "*a newt*"[3] – in this case, dialect preserves the more etymologically correct form of the word.

Other examples may be found in only partial or sporadic dialect use, for example, *oaves*, a dialect variant of StE *eaves*, found throughout most of the South-West including central Wiltshire – the informant at Netheravon added: "they 'ouldn't zay *eaves*, they'd zay *oaves*, th' ol' men" – and this widespread South-Western feature (*ovvis* or *offis* is said still to mean *edge* in Somerset dialect)[4] has led philologists to recognise that alongside the recorded OE *efes*, there must also have been a variant **ofes*.[5] Usually considered a "corruption" of the "correct" form, dialect *wopse*, StE *wasp*, may, however, reflect the original main OE form, *wæps*, whereas the standard language has adopted the OE variant *wæsp*. (The South-Western form was taken to Newfoundland – see DNE under *wop*).

DIFFERENT WORDS OF THE SAME MEANING

In the previous paragraph we have discussed pairs of words of native stock which are really the same word in slightly variant guises, but equally, there are similar pairs of words of native stock that are quite unrelated etymologically (however beguilingly similar they may appear at first sight, compare *afraid* and *afeared*, above), where dialect favours a different word from that used in StE, though it may be familiar enough to the StE speaker: such a pair are dialect *fowls* v. StE *hens*. It could further be claimed that dialect has made creative use of its conservatism in this instance, by preserving a useful SEMANTIC distinction (i.e. one of meaning) that StE has lost: the StE use of *hens* generalises the word that more strictly applies to the female of the domesticated species, and thus has laid itself open to confusion between *hen* (domesticated fowl) and *hen* (female bird). Another pair, superficially similar but not COGNATE (etymologically related), are dialect *clout* v. StE *cloth* (occurring in SED, *dish-cloth/clout*); *clout* is mainly a North Country (NCy) form, but otherwise partially South-Western, being found in Dorset, most of Wiltshire and western parts of Somerset and Hampshire.

43

A clearly regional word is dialect *furze*, corresponding to StE *gorse*. The present distribution of the names shows *furze* as a purely Southern word, except in Berkshire, East Kent, Gloucestershire and North-West Wiltshire, which, with the rest of Central England as far north as Yorkshire, have *gorse* (the far North and Norfolk, both areas heavily settled by the Danes, now have *whin*, of Scandinavian origin).[6] From the evidence of place-names it is clear that the *furze* area must have extended further north in earlier times: note *Furzenhill*[7] and *Furze Platt*, Berkshire, and *Freseley*, Warwickshire. It is interesting to note that the place-name *Gorsey Leaze* (Norton), the only name containing this element according to PNW in Wiltshire, falls in the north-west of the county, and though only recorded since 1820, does seem to imply that in this area the boundary has been fairly stationary.

An interesting pair of words of this type is used as the name of the threshing-implement, StE *flail* (from OE **flegil*, late OE *fligil*, an adoption of the Latin word *flagellum*, its later Middle English currency being probably due to reinforcement from Old French *flaiel, fleel*). From its history, this word deserves to be considered not so much native as naturalised. The native word, dialect *threshel*, metathesised from OE *therscel*, is found in South Wiltshire (in the form *draishl, drIshl*), Somerset, Cornwall, and West Devon, and a small enclave in parts of Herefordshire and Shropshire, and is known also in Worcestershire and Gloucestershire – it is clearly on the retreat (the technical term is RECESSIVE) before *flail*, which otherwise holds the country: an example of a word whose range must at one time have been nationwide, whose distribution in the fifties seems to represent the remnants of an area restricted in the nineteenth century to the South-West, and which by now, with the passing of the implement itself, is possibly extinct.

Another place-name element formerly in general StE use is South-West dialect (though not Devon and Cornwall) *ground*, in the sense now conveyed by StE *field*, but which survives in the standard language in the sense of "the land

44

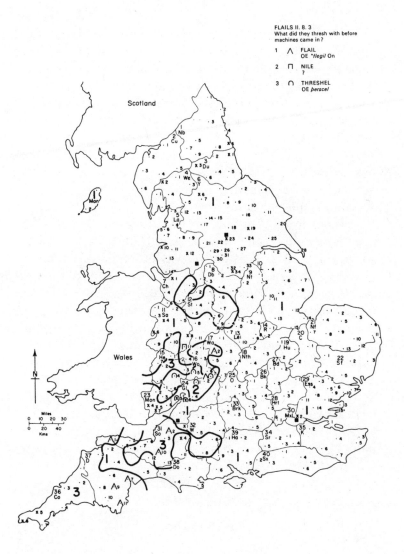

10 *Map showing the distribution of words for* flails *as recorded in SED (after WGE). Wiltshire is on the boundary of the* flail *and* threshel *areas, the south of the county preserving the word of Germanic stock, the rest of the county, like the bulk of the country, using the OE word of Romance origin.*

belonging to a (large) house, park", for example, in the expression "house and grounds".[8] The editor of the EPNE suggested that the distribution of the OE element *grund* in field-names from Middle English times onwards in the sense, *field*, may well be due to the Scandinavian settlement (ON had identical words having this sense), but he admits that the Old English word could mean a *stretch of land*, and in late Old English an *outlying farm, outlying fields*, and it seems unlikely that if such had, indeed, been the case, the word should survive in dialect exclusively in the un-Scandinavianised South-West.[9]

Another interesting pair are dialect *barm*, StE *yeast*; StE *yeast* is recorded only once in (late) Old English, and then not again until 1530, when it was probably re-inforced by cognate words in the Low German dialects (note the forms *Dutch yeast* and *German yeast* recorded by SED from Lincolnshire and Essex); *barm*, however, is found in continuous standard use until the nineteenth century, by which time it was already retreating into dialect speech. The informant at Avebury who knew both words, remarked that *barm* was "older". (*Barm* has, however, been preserved in Newfoundland, see DNE.) *Learn* in the sense of StE *teach*, is general in dialect and, indeed, of venerable antiquity in Standard English, being found from *c*.1200, and used quite normally by Shakespeare, Bunyan, and other "classic" writers of StE into the twentieth century.

Foreign Imports Accepted into Dialect

We have seen above that the standard language has borrowed many words from foreign languages down the centuries: *mole* from a Low German dialect; *viper, perch, afraid* (and *brush* and *beak*) from French, *pus* and *vomit* from (medical) Latin; and *awn* and *stack* from Old Norse, and that dialect has resisted the foreign import and retained a word of often great antiquity from the native Old English stock.

46

There are, however, rare instances – the exceptions that prove the rule – where the reverse is true, for example, StE *pluck* (a chicken), dialect *pick*, and StE *rung* (of a ladder), dialect *round*; here, both the dialect words derive from French.

Occasionally when a foreign word has been borrowed into StE, it has also been accepted by dialect, and because of the very conservatism we have already noted (that, for example, has preserved words from Old English lost to the standard language) has preserved the foreign word in a form closer to its original guise than the standard language, which has fully naturalised it by applying the normal linguistic changes to it: such a word is *mushroom*, from Old French *mousseron*, stressed on the last of its three syllables. Throughout Wiltshire, the trisyllabic form is preserved, as well as the final -*n*, and in three cases (at Avebury, Steeple Ashton and Fovant) the Old French stress on the third syllable is also preserved, i.e. dialect *musheróon*.

One small but interesting group of foreign imports into Wiltshire dialect are those that can be shown to be of Welsh origin. Excluding place-names (see Chapter 5) the number of proven imports into English of Celtic origin is, in fact, extremely small (excepting, of course, the English of former Celtic-speaking areas such as Cornwall), and even these few are hardly StE vocabulary. One such is *brock*, the oldest "English" word for *badger*, OE *broc(c)*, formerly in fairly common use, an early loan from Primitive Welsh **brocc*, later *broch*;[10] SED found only one example in our South-West area (at Ansty in Dorset), and D&G do not record it, but it does survive in Wiltshire in the place-name, *Brock*lees Farm, near Corsham, from OE *brocca léah*, i.e. *badgers' wood/clearing* (see PNW).

A word that is certainly of Welsh origin is dialect *tallet*, StE *hay-loft*, recorded by SED in Wiltshire only in the extreme south of the county at Fovant, though to judge from D&G, formerly of much wider distribution, deriving from Welsh *taflod*. The distribution map confirms the suggested Welsh

HAY-LOFT I.3.18

Where do you store your hay, if you
have it inside (the cow-house)?

1 ∧ HAY-LOFT
OE *hēg*+LOE
loft a ON *loft*
*1573

2 ⊓ TALLET
Welsh *taflod*
1586

Scotland

Man

Wales

Miles
0 10 20 30
0 20 40
Kms

N

11 *Map showing the distribution of words for* hay-loft *as recorded in SED (after WGE). The extreme south of the county is included in the area of Britain in which* tallet *is used and confirms the suggested derivation of the word and the building from Wales.*

origin, the word *tallet* being found in a curved area extending from the counties bordering Wales, throughout the South-Western counties as far as Cornwall. Wakelin suggests that this comparatively recently attested word in English (first OED citation 1586) entered the language via the Welsh cattle-drovers on their way to cattle markets.[11]

Another word of Welsh origin, possibly via the same channel, is dialect *tump*, StE *hillock, knoll*; in the nineteenth century, D&G recorded the word in this sense for both North and South Wiltshire (and wanty-*tump* in their 1932 Addenda) plus the derived adjective, *tumpy*, for North Wiltshire, but it is clearly recessive now, being recorded only twice in Wiltshire by SED, in the sense *tussock*, at Steeple Ashton, found only once otherwise in Worcestershire, and in the compound *emmet-tump*, StE *ant-hill*.[12] Further, PNW notes that in the Melksham area "fields called Tumps have many knolls" (several of this name are recorded on the *c*.1840 Tithe Award Map), and there is the prehistoric barrow, site of the hundred meeting-place at Swanborough *Tump*, near Pewsey.[13] Here again, the early spelling, *toomp* (in Owen's *Pembrokeshire* of 1603), and the frequent West Midlands pronunciation, *tump* (with the *u* sound in *bush*), both point to the vowel sound of Welsh *twmp*, and the distribution – Welsh border counties, Gloucestershire, East Somerset and North Wiltshire – clinches the matter.

A final word of possible Welsh origin is *cam-*, in dialect *cam-handed*, recorded from Sutton Benger, in the sense, StE *left-handed*. (Recorded in this sense for North Wiltshire by D&G who also list the simplex, *cam*, as meaning *perverse, cross*, and cite two instances from Akerman's stories.) Welsh *cam* has the general meaning *crooked, distorted, awry*, as well as such specific meanings as *hunch-backed*, and *squint-/ one-eyed* (though it must be admitted, not the sense *left-handed* or *clumsy*), and is highly productive of compounds of the type which in English have the prefix, *mis-* or *dis-*.[14] Against this proposed derivation (followed by OED and *The Oxford dictionary of English etymology* (ODEE)), it must, however, be admitted that the present distribution, including the *gammy-*[15] examples, is not supportive of such a conclusion (note *cam* and *cam-crooked* in Newfoundland – DNE).

The distribution-map is an important category of evidence when dealing with etymologies – we have already seen how the distribution of dialect *ground* in the sense, StE *field*, belies the suggested Scandinavian origin; another such word is dialect *athwart* (adverb and preposition), StE *diagonally*, found at Ashton Keynes, Sutton Benger, Steeple Ashton, and Fovant (in the form *athurt*), and *thwart*, found at Ashton Keynes, Burbage, and Netheravon (in the form *thurt*), both said to derive from ON *thvert*. (also recorded by DNE as used in Newfoundland). WGE, however, shows these words to be found exclusively in the South-West, the area of England most remote from Scandinavian influence and certainly never settled by Scandinavians. What is more, the words are not even found in the areas known to have been settled by Scandinavians! The present-day distribution of this word in dialect should prompt us to reject the suggested ON etymology, and look, rather, for possible derivation from the cognate OE *thwe(o)rh* with INORGANIC (redundantly added) *-t*,[16] or, more likely, via the phonetic development of final OE *h* to *θ* to *t*. In the same phonetic environment, D&G record *steert* as a form of *steer* with inorganic *-t* (from OE *stēor*). (Inorganic *-d* after final *-r* is fairly common in South-Western dialect: D&G instance *millerd* and *scholard*. SED records *dillerd* from Wiltshire for *shaft-horse*, i.e. *thiller*; compare also, after medial *-r*, *wurden* in Appendix 3, The Cannings Vawk.) Dialect *durns*, StE *jambs*, is assumed to be related to Norwegian *dyrn* by the dictionaries, but is found mainly in the South-West (including South Wiltshire), and may well be another word where we should look for an Old English cognate, or where one may have to be postulated.[17]

One word where Wiltshire dialect *does* show a borrowing form Old Norse, is dialect *grain*, StE *tine, prong* (the former

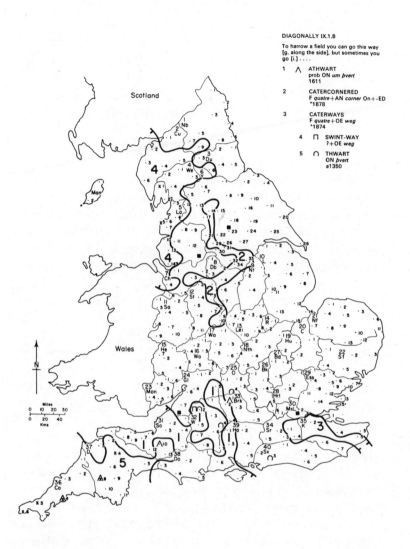

DIAGONALLY IX.1.8

To harrow a field you can go this way
[g. along the side], but sometimes you
go [i.] . . . .

1	∧	**ATHWART** prob ON *um þvert* 1611
2		**CATERCORNERED** F *quatre* + AN *corner* On + -ED *1878
3		**CATERWAYS** F *quatre* + OE *weg* *1874
4	⊓	**SWINT-WAY** ? + OE *weg*
5	∩	**THWART** ON *þvert* a1350

12 *Map showing the distribution of words for* diagonally *as recorded in SED (after WGE). Note that* (a)thwart *is only found in the south west of the country, an area not settled by the Norse, which tends to discredit the suggested ON etymology and perhaps favours a native OE coinage (see p. 50).*

51

is the Old English word), found also in neighbouring Hampshire and Berkshire, and otherwise throughout North-West England (an area of Norse settlement): here, the WGE distribution-map shows a break between the two areas only as wide as the extent of Worcestershire, and we may assume that the area was earlier unbroken; (recorded also for Newfoundland by DNE).[18] Another such word, is dialect *gilt* (from ON *gyltr*), v. dialect *yeld* (from OE *g(i)elde*) although neither word, meaning *young sow*, could claim to be StE, belonging rather to the specialist vocabulary of agriculture, where *gilt* may be said to hold most of the country and was found in that form once in Wiltshire, at Netheravon, at the extreme western point of its south-eastern distribution; the rest of the county seems to show retention of the archaic native form.

SUBJECT AREAS

Introduction

Mention of the vocabulary of agriculture prompts us to consider the areas of vocabulary to which many dialect words belong. The editors of SED deliberately set out to study the kind of dialect "normally spoken by elderly speakers [almost without exception, men: "in this country men speak vernacular more frequently, more consistently, and more genuinely than women"] of 60 years of age or over belonging to the same social class in rural communities, and in particular by those who were, or had formerly been, employed in farming, for it is amongst the rural populations that the traditional types of vernacular English are best preserved today." As a result, it is hardly surprising that a large proportion of the words recorded in SED that strike a speaker of StE as curious, should belong to the vocabulary of rural or farming life, and we shall pass on now to a consideration of those words especially which describe things peculiar to such life in our area. Naturally, a large number of these words are concerned with animals: we have already looked at *want, emmet, evet, brock* and *fowl*, which are merely different words used by dialect speakers to denote animals familiar enough by other names to speakers of StE, but now we shall consider specialist names of the *gilt* type.

The Agricultural Lexicon

ANIMAL NAMES AND TERMS OF ANIMAL HUSBANDRY

Staying with pigs for a moment, there is an entertaining group of words to describe the smallest pig or *runt* of the litter: geographically, Wiltshire lies in a transitional area between *dilling* and related words to the north-east, and *nestle-tripe* to the south-west. To deal with the other words first: *squeaker* from Burbage is transparent enough, though, interestingly, first recorded in this sense by OED in Dickens's *Great expectations. Rinnick* from Ashton Keynes and Sutton Benger is also found to the north-west in Gloucestershire, and is taken by the editors of the *Word geography of England* to be a form of the north-country *reckling* and its variants (there is only a relatively narrow tract of the equally etymologically obscure *nisgal* between the two words). *Darrel* (from Whiteparish), *dorrel* (from Burbage), and *darling* (from Avebury and Netheravon; a folk-etymology?) are probably all variants of the similarly obscure *dilling*,[19] as is *daniel* (which we heard used locally as the nickname of a man not so christened, and explained as referring to the fact that he was the youngest and smallest child of a large family!). *Nestle-tripe* is an interesting word (Steeple Ashton, Sutton Veny, Fovant), it too was taken to Newfoundland where, however, it has come to mean a *naughty child!*[20]

Only in South Somerset and South Wiltshire is the word *chilver* any longer found in English; it is used to denote a *new-born female lamb* at Sutton Veny, and such a *lamb up to the time of its first shearing* at Netheravon and Fovant; after the Old English period the word is not found again until it

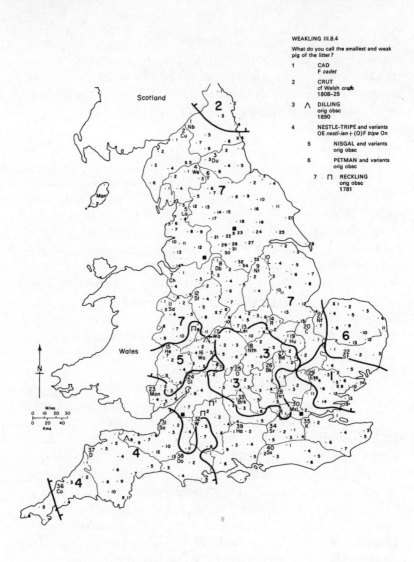

WEAKLING III.8.4

What do you call the smallest and weak pig of the litter?

1		CAD
		F *cadet*
2		CRUT
		cf Welsh *cruh*
		1808–25
3	∧	DILLING
		orig obsc
		1890
4		NESTLE-TRIPE and variants
		OE *nestl-ian* + (O)F *tripe* On
5		NISGAL and variants
		orig obsc
6		PETMAN and variants
		orig obsc
7	⊓	RECKLING
		orig obsc
		1781

13 *Map showing the distribution of words for* runt *as recorded in SED (after WGE). The south of the county belongs to the south-western* nestle-tripe *area, while the rest of the county shows a variety of response.*

54

turns up in the early nineteenth century dialect records – quietly preserved by South-Western dialect for over 800 years!

A dehorned cow is known as a *not(-cow)* in much of Wiltshire, as elsewhere, in South West England, deriving from OE *hnot, clipped, shorn*; another word of more general dialect distribution, is *poll(-cow)*, from Steeple Ashton, i.e. *polled*. (See D&G under *polly, a pollarded tree* (South Wiltshire).) Alongside StE *heifer* for a cow past the stage of being a calf, Sutton Veny and Fovant preserve *stirk*, another word of Old English derivation, now a North-West England dialect word (though earlier recorded by D&G for North Wiltshire in their 1932 Addenda). Dialect also has a word to describe a male horse only half-castrated, a *rig* in Southern England, a *ridgel* further north. A final specialised animal word, no longer to be found with the general disappearance of the heavy horse as a means of motive power, is that for a *shaft-horse*, dialect *thiller* (mostly *diller* in Wiltshire, but see above).

Moving on now from specialised animal words to more general animal names, *donkey* has now superseded the earlier StE *ass* (doubtless because it began to coincide in sound with the taboo word, *arse*) as the StE word, though seemingly itself a dialect word of East Anglian origin. Several of the names for this animal seem to testify to a (grudging) affection: *donkey* is itself probably a pet-form of the personal name, *Duncan* (earlier it rhymed with *monkey*): *cuddy* in the far north of England, of *Cuthbert* (the local saint); *neddy*, a familiar child's name for the animal (and found just over the Wiltshire border at Weston in Somerset), of *Edward*, and *dicky* (East Anglian), of *Richard*. Two other names are recorded from Wiltshire: *nirrup* from Whiteparish and neighbouring parts of Hampshire and Dorset only, is quite obscure, but *moke* from Fovant may possibly be ultimately (as *moggy*, for a calf or cow, and now, generally, for a cat is probably also) a pet-form of *Margaret* (though note how all the other pet-names are male).[21] *Looty* which we

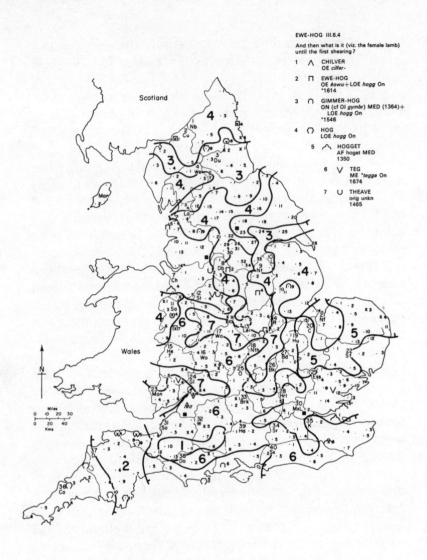

14 *Map showing the distribution of words for* ewe-hog *(a female lamb before its first shearing) as recorded in SED (after WGE). The south of the county is part of the very small area of the country which preferred* chilver, *a word not otherwise attested since OE times.*

have noted in an early nineteenth century manuscript glossary of Wiltshire words, is also obscure and probably obsolete
by now. *Reynolds* from Burbage as a familiar name for the
fox, has a venerable history in English from as far back as the
fourteenth century poem, *Sir Gawayne & the Green Knight*,
and was popularised originally by the dissemination of the
thirteenth century fable of *Reynard the Fox*.

"What do you call that small kind of mouse with the long
snout; it eats insects and lives outside?" SED labels this
animal *shrewmouse* (as did the informant at Sutton Veny):
its more colourful names are *shearcrop* from Fovant (D&G
recorded this from Baverstock), and *harvest-row* from
Sutton Benger and Burbage. (Found in the form *harvest-
trow* in Jefferies; which we have heard in the form, *archtrow*
from an informant in Alton Barnes. The *-row* is pronounced
as in "row of beans" but we wonder whether this is not
simply a corruption of **harvest-shrew*.) Another name for
this animal attested as current in *Whitlock's Wessex* (1975),
but also much earlier (in Maton's *Natural history of a part of
the county of Wiltshire* (1843) where it antedates OED's first
citation) is *overrunner*; the *Hampshire dialect glossary* (1883)
comments, "which is supposed to portend ill-luck if it runs
over a person's foot." Compare, from the 1545 edition of Sir
Thomas Elyot's *Latin-English dictionary*, under *Mus araneus*: "a kynde of myse called a shrew, whyche yf it goo over
a beastes backe, he shall be lame in the chyne" (i.e. Modern
English *chine*, the back bone).[22] Which came first, the folk-
belief or the folk-etymology?

StE *bat* was also known as *batmouse* at Avebury, Burbage
and Fovant and as *raremouse* at Netheravon; OED describes
the bat as a "mouse-like quadruped" and this accounts for
the second element in these names, as well as in dialect *flitter-
mouse*, German *Fledermaus*, and French *chauve-souris*,
literally, "bald-mouse". It is not certain what the first element in the Netheravon form means (see OED under *rear-
mouse, reremouse* deriving from late OE *hreremūs*), but
nineteenth century students of Wiltshire dialect, for

example, Akerman and Britton, recorded the pronunciation *ryemouse* which probably preserves a form of the word closer to the earlier attested OE *hrēathemūs*, with the same meaning.

StE *tadpole* is composed of *toad* + *poll* (= *head*, compare *poll(-cow)* above), as if the creature were a "toad that is all head"; two Wiltshire words recorded by SED are *catpole* (Sutton Benger and Steeple Ashton), probably merely a corruption of *tadpole*, brought about by the folk-etymological process of trying to make sense of the no longer understood first element, *tad-*, and *tomgudgeon* (Ashton Keynes); compare *tom(my)-toddy* (SED, Cornwall and Devon); *tomthumbs* (Devon); D&G record *Tom Cull* as a Wiltshire name for the *bullhead* (itself a common dialect word for *tadpole*, and also known popularly as *miller's thumb*, compare *tomthumb* above); EDD records *tom carse* as another, and *Tom barsey* (perhaps merely a variant of the previous) for *sticklecback*; we need not doubt, therefore, that *tomgudgeon* is the StE word, *gudgeon*, a small freshwater fish, prefaced by the familiar personal name, *Tom*, as in the foregoing examples.

Kindle (down) is a specialised word in general use throughout most of the country (recorded by SED for Wiltshire at Ashton Keynes, Burbage, and Fovant), meaning (*of rabbits*) *give birth*: formerly more widely known, compare Shakespeare's *As You Like It*, "As the cony that you see dwell where she is kindled" (III.ii.358), the word is now preserved in dialect. (For the etymology, compare German *Kind, child*.)

The SED Questionnaire devotes a complete section of its Book 3 to the words for the noises animals are said to make, and for human cries used to call animals. As examples of the former, we may mention: for StE *bellow, blare* from Fovant (used for StE *moo* just south of the border in Dorset, used of cows and moose (!) in its new Newfoundland home: see DNE); *bawl* is used for *moo* at Steeple Ashton, Sutton Veny, and Fovant (and when taken to Newfoundland used for the young seal's cry). In StE *blare* is now only used of the sound made by trumpets (or similar, for example, car-horns), but this usage is only recorded from the late eighteenth century by OED; it is used of cows, however, as far back as Coverdale's *Bible* translation of 1535. "How do you call ducks in from the field?" The call to be repeated to Wiltshire ducks is *dill(y)*, found first in a nursery rhyme called *Mrs. Bond*: "John Ostler go fetch me a duckling or two; Cry, dilly, dilly, dilly, dilly, come and be killed", hauntingly alluded to in Dylan Thomas's *Over Sir John's Hill* (recorded too by DNE under *dill*).

Flush(ed) was used at Steeple Ashton, Sutton Veny and Fovant, for StE *fledged*, a word recorded by OED (under *flush* adj.3) in the early seventeenth century, and then not again until John Britton's *Beauties of Wiltshire* (1825) (see also Appendix 3, Stoopid Owld Wosbird).

South Wiltshire uses a South-Western dialect word, *pin-bone*, for the *hip-bone of a cow*, hip-bone being reserved in the South for human reference (though note *huckle-bone* from Fovant). There is a special word too for the "*inner layer of fat round the kidneys of a pig*", i.e. *flick*, found throughout the South-West except Cornwall;[23] so too, for the "*lungs, liver and heart of a slaughtered animal*" i.e. *hinge, (h)enge.*[24]

THE FARM AND FARM-LIFE

Shard (from Burbage and Steeple Ashton) for a *gap in a hedge to let sheep through* recorded in that sense from Old English times, is now only dialect (it occurs in the form *shurde* in the sixteenth and seventeenth century *Calne Guild Stewards' Book*[25]). *Staple* is the word used to denote the *stake to which an animal (for example, a cow) is tethered* – an extraordinary dialect survival of a sense which OED considered obsolete and for which its last citation is 1387! (compare also *long-staple* from Somerset). Incidentally, the same word in the sense, *post, stake*, can be found in Wiltshire place-names, for example, *Staple*ford is the *ford marked by a post*, and *Staple* Hundred, whose meeting-place was presumably marked by some notable wooden column, the site of which is probably preserved in the field named *Steeple* Piece, just north of Purton Church.[26]

Cow-shed (and *cow-house*) are now the StE words for the building in which cows are kept, yet the former is not recorded until as late as 1886, in an Act of Parliament, which quite reasonably leads the editors of WGE to conjecture that "quite likely . . . it has been spread by government literature and officials". The Old English words seem to have been *byre* (mainly Northern), and *shippen* (of more general distribution until later replaced by *cow-house*), recorded for North-West England and Devon, and neighbouring parts of Cornwall and Somerset by SED, a distribution which shows that the word was formerly in use over the whole of Western England at least, as is confirmed by place-name evidence, compare *Shippon*, Berkshire, and Puck*shipton* (Beechingstoke, near Pewsey, Wiltshire).[27] Two other words recorded from Wiltshire were *cow-barken* (from Sutton Benger), and (*cow-*)*skillin'* (from central Wiltshire). At Avebury and Burbage, a *skillin'* was defined as having "one open side". This word, formerly of much wider distribution (see EDD under *skeeling*), is now restricted solely to Wiltshire, though, in the sense *cart-shed*, it was found by SED in two localities in neighbouring Berkshire. *Cow-barken* (and *rick-barken* for *rick-yard*, from Ashton Keynes, Steeple Ashton and Netheravon) is the only survival recorded for Wiltshire in SED of a word formerly common throughout the South-West (WGE shows it now only in central Somerset and West Dorset), in the sense, *farmyard*, i.e. *barton* or *barken*, compare *Barton* Farm, Bradford-on-Avon, and the *Barton* (locally, *Barken*), the name of a group of cottages in Clyffe Pypard – D&G under *barken* state, "*barton* was formerly in very common use, but has now [i.e. *c.*1890] been replaced by *yard*", and compare Skinner's 1671 *Etymological dictionary*: "a word in very common use in the county of Wiltshire, *atrium*, a yard of a house"; and Bishop Kennett's *Parochial antiquities* (1695): "now commonly used for a yard or backside in Wiltshire and other counties . . ."

15 *Mr and Mrs Gally Bagger. The original and his female counterpart discovered in a Pewsey allotment. Gally-bagger is one of the several fascinating English dialect words for the scarecrow, of uniquely south-western distribution: the first element is the semantic equivalent of 'scare' and the second element belongs to the family of 'bogey' words.*

To move on now to consider rural words not directly related to animal husbandry; there is a fascinating series of words in English dialect for StE *scarecrow*; in South Wiltshire the word is *gallybagger*, found otherwise only in adjoining parts of Hampshire. It is first recorded by the Wiltshireman, John Britton, in 1825 (in fact, as an Isle of Wight word), who gives *gally-crow* as a Wiltshire form. (*Dolly-crow*, from Steeple Ashton and two localities in Dorset, is doubtless a folk-etymologising form, replacing the obscure first element, *gally-*, with a more readily understandable, and not irrelevant, word.) *Gallied*, for StE *scared, frightened*, was found by SED only at two localities in Dorset, but it was recorded by D&G under *gally, gallow*; the word derives from OE *-gælwan*, but is not subsequently recorded by OED before *King Lear* (1605) (taken to Newfoundland see DNE under *gally*). The second element (sometimes folk-etymologised to *-beggar*, doubtless on account of the scarecrow's dress)[28] is (the mainly North Country) *boggart*, a *spectre, goblin, bogey* (of which last word it is a variant),[29] as can be shown from the similar formation, "a *frayboggarde* in a garden off Cucumbers", in Coverdale's 1525 *Bible* translation. *Mommet*, from Ashton Keynes, found otherwise by SED only in West Somerset and a small part of Devon, is OED *maumet* sense 2, "an image, dressed-up figure; a doll, puppet; also a person of grotesque appearance or costume, a guy", ultimately deriving from the name of the prophet, *Mahomet*, due to the mistaken Medieval notion that he was worshipped as an idol by Moslems. The last word to be considered, *udmidud*, from Sutton Benger (D&G under *hudmedud* (1)), was otherwise found by SED only once in the south of the country, in neighbouring Berkshire. OED records this under *hodmandod*,[30] as being first found in the late nineteenth-century dialect glossaries, but we are fortunate in having much earlier evidence for this sense from our own area, in a late seventeenth-century compendium of folk-lore entitled, *Remaines of Gentilisme and Judaisme* by the famous Wiltshire antiquary,

John Aubrey: "Hodmendods in gardens, that is likenesse of men to scare birds".[31] D&G (though not SED) also record *hodmedod* as meaning snail, and this is, indeed, the earliest attested sense in OED (from 1626)[32]: here is a riddle in semantics! Why is a scarecrow like a snail? How could the one meaning develop from the other? The solution seems to be as follows; OED suggests *hodmandod* (compare the slightly earlier attested form, *hoddydod*) is a "nursery reduplication" (i.e. a childish part-rhyming formation of the *handy-dandy*, *bow-wow*, *piggy-wig*, type) of *dodman*, a word meaning snail, found from *c.*1550 (Dickens uses it as a dialect word in *David Copperfield*). There is a similar sounding but unrelated word, *dudman*, first recorded in 1674 in OED in the sense, *scarecrow*, found by SED in neighbouring Oxfordshire, and recorded from Malmesbury by D&G in the last century. With this additional evidence we are now in a position to postulate the following development taking place probably in the late seventeenth century; when *hodmandod* had developed as a part-rhyming-variant of *dodman* (i.e. in its original sense, *snail*), because of the assumed identity of this word with the existing *dudman* (=*scare-crow*) on account of their similar sound, *hodmandod* was also naturally regarded as having the sense, *scarecrow*.[33]

Another interesting group consists of the words for a *between-meals snack*, and for a *meal taken to work*, among which there was found some overlap as discussed in the examples below.

Dewbit was only recorded once for Wiltshire, in the extreme south-east at Whiteparish where it was described as "taken by the mowers after about an hour's work at 5 a.m."; SED found it otherwise only in neighbouring Hampshire, at Hatherden, but reference to EDD will show that it was formerly widespread throughout the southern counties – clearly another example of the word disappearing from the lexicon, with the disappearance of the thing or custom it refers to. The element -*bit* appears in this word in its original etymological sense of a "*bite* to eat", and is probably so used in the responses recorded from elsewhere in the south, of the type, *a bit of crib/lunch/bait*.

Nammet derives ultimately from OE *nōnmete*, i.e. *meat* eaten at *noon*, preserving the old, more general sense of *meat* meaning *food*, still found in certain fossilised expressions in StE such as *meat and drink*. In their 1899 Addenda D&G report that "About Salisbury ... Nammet is at 12" (i.e. noon according to our modern reckoning). *Noonmeat* had fallen out of StE use by *c*.1600, but was preserved in dialect where it first surfaces again in Jennings's *Obsolete dialect of the West of England* (1825), in the form, *nummet*. Another word, mainly recorded from Wiltshire only, in the sense, *mid-morning snack* (and at Fovant, said to consist simply of bread and cheese), is *nuncheon, nunch*. *Nuncheon* is from ME *nōn-schench*, the counterpart of *nōn-mete*, i.e. *drink at noon*, and is defined by OED as "a slight refreshment of liquor etc., originally taken in the afternoon..." (because the earliest meaning of *noon* was not *12 o'clock, mid-day*, but about 3 p.m.), so that it is of interest to note that D&G go on to report that "about Salisbury", *nuncheon* is taken mid-morning, "and again at 4 p.m. and is a very small meal, merely a piece of bread and a glass of beer." (*Nunch* in the sense *between-meals snack* is also recorded from Newfoundland, see DNE.)

Lunch from Ashton Keynes, Sutton Benger, Burbage and Netheravon, was used in the sense of *mid-morning snack*, especially of bread and cheese, and this preserves the original seventeenth century time of the meal, and the earliest sense of the word, which means *hunk*, and was used especially of a hunk of bread and cheese (*lunch* in the wider sense of *between-meals snack* is again recorded from Newfoundland – DNE).

We move on now to consider some words related to harvest and haymaking: "What is your word for putting sheaves together in the harvest field for drying?" asked SED. The most common response, especially in the southern half of the county, is *hiling*, a word found also in neighbouring East

Dorset and West Hampshire but nowhere else in England.[34] "When you put the drying hay into small heaps, for example, overnight in case of rain, what do you call them?" *Pooks*, the main response, is a distinctly South-Western word, compare OED's citation from Lisle's *Husbandry* (*a.*1722), "In making the wheat-pooks in Wiltshire, the sheaves . . .', and a sixteenth-century example of the verb from a Wiltshire Rent Roll. (*Pook* was another word taken to Newfoundland from the South-West dialect – see DNE.) *Mow* meaning *hay-stack* is recorded by SED for neighbouring East Somerset, Gloucestershire, and Monmouthshire, but was not found in this sense in Wiltshire (but compare *wind mow* as recently as D&G's 1932 Addenda for a small haycock), except in the derived sense, *hayloft*, at Burbage.[35] We are probably all familiar with the word *swath* for a *row of mown grass*, general throughout Wiltshire, but at Sutton Benger *wake* was recorded, perhaps a metaphorical transfer of the nautical usage. At two localities in neighbouring Gloucestershire, SED recorded *wally* ("*wolly*"), noted, under *wallow*, for North Wiltshire by D&G. In Richard Jefferies's day, at least, a subtle distinction between the sense of the two words was preserved: "Watching that the 'wallows' may be turned over properly, and the 'wakes' made at a just distance from each other" (*Wild life in a southern county*, 1879). Nowadays, we are only really familiar with the word, *aftermath*, in its figurative sense, *consequence, outcome*, but as the response, *aftergrass*, from Steeple Ashton, makes clear, originally it refers to a second mowing or crop of grass. *Lattermath* was received from North Wiltshire, compare Jefferies again: "The aftermath, or, as country people call it, the 'latter-math'" (*Round about a great estate*, 1880). The word for a *portion of hay cut from the rick ready for use*, gives us two nouns from the verbs *carve* and *cleave*, i.e. *cerf* (D&G under *kerf*), which OED could not find before Halliwell's 1847 dialect glossary, though it is probably to be understood in the *kyrffe* of the mainly seventeenth century *Calne Guild Stewards' Book*, and *clef* (see D&G's 1899 Addenda).

16 *"Nammet" at Workway Drove, Alton Priors, October 1939.*

The *ridges* of a ploughed field, sometimes pronounced *rudges* in Wiltshire, were known at Avebury and Burbage as *verins* (compare OED under *feerin* and D&G under *veer*); at the latter, the informant declared it to be "the proper name". *Feer-* is apparently simply a variant development of OE *furh*, modern *furrow*, so it looks as if it is a case of the main form, *furrow*, being retained in its original sense, and the variant, *feering*, being used for the continuation of the furrow, i.e. the *ridge*.[36] (Another example, incidentally, of a word being preserved in dialect: after one citation for the verb, *feer*, *c*.1400, the word is not recorded again by OED until 1800.)

An ancient craft such as thatching naturally has its own specialist vocabulary, and the pegs used to fasten down thatch are known either as *spicks* or *spars*; D&G regarded the two words as identical in use, but SED's informant at Avebury explained that *spicks* were used for thatching ricks, *spars* for house-roofs. In a slightly Latinised form, *spica*, it is found in this sense as early as the late thirteenth century *Accounts* of Adam de Stratton.[37]

The Child's Lexicon

SED does not really concern itself with children's usage, but terms current in the fifties, at least, and probably still so, may be found in Iona & Peter Opie's *The lore and language of schoolchildren* (1959).

The "truce-term" is a very important item in the child's vocabulary: *cree* is the term used in North Wiltshire (also noted by EDD), presumably a shortened form of *creases* recorded from Wantage (Berks), and the Oxfordshire *cruces*; *crosses* from further north makes plain the etymology, the term doubtless deriving from the making of the sign of the cross, even if only in the somewhat diluted form of crossing one's fingers.

The most interesting truce-term, however, is the *fainites* or *fains* from South Wiltshire (doubtless forms with the expected initial *v* sound occur in Wiltshire, but, as the Opies say, "children are often uncertain whether the word begins with an *f* or a *v* – expostulating that they have never before been asked to spell it!"), which this part of our county shares with the greater part of southern England. The word is a form of StE *feign* in the Middle English sense, *"avoid, shirk doing something, hang back (from battle)"*[38], not recorded after 1535, but, astonishingly, preserved in children's usage since that date.[39]

From the Avon valley the Opies record the child's technical term for ensuring the avoidance of some unpleasant task, it is to shout *"moans"*! (the direct opposite of the widespread *"bags"*): "This mournful cry seems, however, to be confined to the east bank of the river, to Durnford, Netton, and Salterton. On the west bank, at Lake, Wilsford, and Upper, Middle, and Lower Woodford, the children are content to be like the majority and shout 'Bags not'."

From the many children's terms of disapproval for other children, the Opies record a Wiltshire word for *"cry-baby"*: "especially in the south-west, a person is said to be *grizzling* when he is merely whining and complaining, the brat himself being styled *grizzle-guts* or, in Wiltshire, *grizzle-grunt"* (cf. D&G s.vv. *grizzle* and *grump*).[40]

Direct study of the child's lexicon provides a useful means of assessing the present state of local dialect. Such a study lends itself particularly to a school-based project and a detailed questionnaire on the child's lexicon, which may be adapted to meet individual requirements, is given in Appendix 4.

The General Lexicon

Moving on now to consider items of more general, non-specialised vocabulary, for example, parts of the body: *clitch* was found for *groin* from Ashton Keynes, but probably meant *crotch* originally[41] (in Newfoundland the word turns up in the form *clitchin*, see DNE). *Quilter* was received from Avebury in both the senses, *throat*, and *windpipe*: D&G

68

17 *Distribution of children's truce-terms, from I. and P. Opie's* The lore and language of schoolchildren, *1959.*

have *quilt* in the sense *swallow (naturally)* – "The baby wur that bad, it couldn't quilt nothen" – and give *glutch* as meaning to *swallow with difficulty*, as well as *glutcher* for *throat*. *Kecker* or *keckhorn* was another word for *windpipe* (and *throat*) formerly current according to D&G, and SED recorded the base of this word, i.e. *keck*, in the sense, *cough*, from Burbage (both *glutch* and *keecorn* are found in Newfoundland, see DNE).[42] StE *cough* is itself a similarly ONOMATOPEIC formation; others recorded by SED are *hackle* and *hawk*, both from Fovant, where the informant defined both as meaning "a short cough". Further evidence of dialect specialisation is provided by *(h)usk*, only used of an animal's cough (D&G note the variant *hask* and *hesk*); OED's first citation for *husky* in this sense is from Edward Lisle's early eighteenth century *Husbandry*: "They have in Wiltshire a disease of their cows which they call a hask or husky cough". *Heckle* was also recorded in this animal sense from Avebury. The word for *torn skin at the root of the finger-nail* is *hangnail* or *agnail* in StE, with original OE *ang-* meaning *painful*, often folk-etymologised to *hang-*; the usual term in Wiltshire is *revelback* or *ravelback* where the etymology seems transparent enough, but from Ashton Keynes and Sutton Benger (and neighbouring Gloucestershire) SED recorded *backfriend*, i.e. a "friend" who hangs back in your time of need, and so is no friend at all! (see OED under *backfriend*, and compare also *backbiter* from various counties, and even *stepmother's blessing* from Derbyshire).

Gipsies are known throughout Wiltshire as *diddikoys*, which according to the OED *Supplement* (under *didicoi, didicoy*) seems to be a Romany word which the gipsies themselves use disparagingly of tinkers.

The numerous words for a *gossip* include *newsbag, newsgag, newspad*, and the Shakespearian *newsmonger* from Fovant. For the action of *gossiping*, the most interesting expression recorded by SED in Wiltshire is *chamragging* and variants (from Burbage and Steeple Ashton), which is clearly an expression parallel to the colloquial *chewing the rag*. (D&G record *cham* from StE *chew*, – "Now cham thee vittles up well" – an older form of StE *champ*, and SED records it throughout neighbouring Berkshire.)

For *head over heels*, the standard Wiltshire expression is *arse over head* (or ... *tip*, from Ashton Keynes), but *pitch-falling* was a response from Avebury, a folk-etymologising version of *pitchpolling* found in neighbouring Gloucestershire, compare D&G "When rooks are flying round and round, playing and tumbling head over heels in the air (a sign of rain), they are said to be 'playing pitch-poll'". (In Newfoundland the *pitchy-paw* is a children's word for a type of common butterfly, doubtless referring to the fluttering manner of its flight, see DNE.)

A word of obscure origin, which escaped inclusion in the original OED,[43] is *dunnikin*, the old-fashioned *earth-closet*; it can, however, be found in DHS under *dunnaken*, etc., where it is traced back as far as the eighteenth century.[44] The earlier meaning of *hovel*, i.e. *shed*, was preserved at Burbage, showing that the domain of this word, Midlands according to SED, must formerly have extended further south.

Two items from the kitchen-garden: *spring-onions*, and *weeds*. The first are known as *gibbles* or *giblets* (pronounced with initial *j*-sound), a distinctly South-Western word. (See OED under *chibol*, and D&G under *chipples*, *cribbles*, and *gibbles*.) A word still to be heard for StE *weeds*, with a delightfully old-fashioned air, is *trumpery* (OED records it in this sense, developed from the general sense, *rubbish*, from the seventeenth century), from Steeple Ashton in "the stubble and all that trumpery". D&G quote from Elisabeth Bayly's *Jonathan Merle: a West Country story of the times* (1890): "If he'd a-let us have it rent free first year ('cause that land wer all full o' trump'ry that high) we could ha' done."

Next, a few words, mostly adjectives, relating to the senses: "if you haven't put enough salt into your food, you say it is...?" *Fresh* is the commonest response (compare StE *freshwater* as opposed to *seawater*). It is pleasing to be able to reassure the editors of the OED here, who found only one citation for *fresh* in this sense[45] from a work published in 1530 and consequently labelled it "Perhaps some error"! In this sense, the word seems limited to South-Western dialect, here is the informant from Burbage: "'tis main fresh; wants zome more zalt". The informant from Netheravon offered the word *mawkish*, significantly a word first recorded in this sense by OED from the Wiltshire antiquary, John Aubrey. Bacon that has gone off is known throughout Wiltshire as *rafty*, a word more or less restricted in its distribution to our county. The verb used to describe the process of putrefaction was *rank* at Whiteparish, a word which OED marks as obsolete, its last citation being from 1606.

A well-known Wiltshire word is *shrammed* (and variants) for *very cold*: in his late eighteenth century glossary, Grose labelled it "Western", and OED quotes from the *Daily Telegraph* for 15th Nov. 1865 – "Being 'shrammed with cold' as they say in Wiltshire" (also current in Newfoundland, see DNE under *scrammed*). This word, along with *shrimpy* and *shrimped up* from Fovant and similar forms[46] constitute a family of words whose earliest known representative is a word found only in late Old English, and even then only once, i.e *scrimman* (pronounced "*shrimman*") meaning *shrivel*, see OED under *shrim*. For *to cool*, South-Western dialect also uses *cold*, a usage first found by OED in Chaucer, but not known after 1600 – another word preserved by our dialect. A child who cannot sit still but is restless or must be up and doing, was labelled *wiggy-arsed* by the informant from Burbage: the first element is perhaps derived from ear*wig*, compare the idiom *to have ants in one's pants*. (A less colourful, and we feel also a less likely, derivation would be from *wiggle*.) Another word is *sprack*, confined to Wiltshire and Somerset, compare "That's a sprack mare o' yourn" from Akerman's *Wiltshire tales* (cited by D&G under *sprack*).

There is a traditional prejudice against left-handed people that is borne out by dialect which, for example, uses the same word for *left-handed* as for *clumsy*, i.e. *cack-/keck-handed*, where the first element is an old taboo word for excrement.[47] Of the other words recorded, we have already noted the pejorative sense of the first element of *cam-/gammy-handed*. *Watty-handed* from Ashton Keynes is a word whose distribution centres on Gloucestershire and its immediate borders (the first element is mysterious).[48] *Marlborough-handed* (only recorded from those places in the neighbourhood of Marlborough, and at Inkpen in Berkshire where it was said to be the "older" word) is now only known in the sense *left-handed,* which however inapplicable it must be to the townspeople as a whole, is at least less offensive than the meaning it had when D&G recorded it: "People who used their tools awkwardly were formerly called *Marlbro-handed vawk*, natives of Marlborough being traditionally famed for clumsiness and unhandiness." It seems this "unhandiness" may be traced back as far as the late twelfth century, when the Herefordshireman, Walter Map, in his book, *De Nugis Curialium* ("Courtiers' Triflings") refers to "French of Marlborough", by which he means *bad* French! With *squippy* and *squiffy* from the south-west of the county, should be compared *skiffy, skivvy, skiffle* and *squivver* from neighbouring parts of Somerset and Dorset only. Both *squiffy* and *swipey* were nineteenth-century slang terms for *slightly drunk*, so the development was no doubt via *clumsy, awkward* (for example, on one's feet, hence the meaning, *splay-footed*, attested in the form, *swippy*, from Sutton Veny) to *left-handed*. (Another Wiltshire word for *splay-footed* is *spraw(l)-footed* which was taken to Newfoundland and used as the uncomplimentary name of a type of grebe – see DNE under *spraw-foot*.)

Lear (also *leary*, as in Hardy) is quite common for *hungry* via its earlier sense, *empty*, which goes back to Old English times. (The anonymous glossarist *c*.1830 writes: "A lear stomach i.e. an empty stomach") (also noted in DNE).)

An interesting group is *clitty*, and *clites* or *clider*: hair that is *tangled* was called *clitty* at Sutton Veny, Fovant and Whiteparish (DNE also records this usage). *Clits* for *tangles* was recorded from Fovant and *clitty* also in the sense, *sad, reluctant to rise*, used of dough. *Clites* (North Wiltshire and adjacent parts of Gloucestershire and Oxfordshire) or *cliders* (rest of the county and Somerset, Hampshire and Devon) is used for *goose-grass*, also known popularly as *cleavers*, because, as Turner explained in his *Herbal* of 1551, "it cleueth vpon mennes clothes." (Grigson[49] also lists for Wiltshire, *beggar lice, clinging sweethearts, kiss-me-quick, lover's knots, sweethearts, traveller's comfort*, and *traveller's ease*.) Clearly the words must all be related, as not only are their forms similar, but they are united by a common meaning, that of stickiness. (See further, the OE place-name element **bors,* ultimately related to the word *burr*, found in *Boseleys* and *Boscombe*, PNW: 361.)

We end this section on the lexicon of Wiltshire dialect with some notable examples of archaism (to add to those noticed above, mostly in passing).

Especially in the south-east of the county, *maid(en)* or *wench* was found in preference to *girl*. *Girl* in the sense of *female child* is surprisingly modern, no unequivocal example being found until *c.*1530 (earlier instances from the late thirteenth century mean simply *child*; the classic example is Shakespeare's *Winters Tale* (III.iii.70).) Unlike *girl, maid* and *wench* are found in Old English.

Betwixt was an alternative to *between* as early as the Old English period, but *between* eventually became exclusive in StE. It was recorded from the informant at Fovant in the phrase "*in betwix' thi teeth*".

Wiltshire lies on the border of the south-eastern area of the country which, like the standard language, uses *autumn* as the name of the season. In the west of the county especially, *fall (of the year)* shows the preference of dialect for such native formations (and one which was, of course, to emigrate to North America and become part of the standard language there. DNE records the full expression *fall of the year* from 1975). Both expressions, however, were relatively new, replacing OE, ME *harvest*; *autumn* not being properly naturalised until the sixteenth century (*fall of the year* is not found until the seventeenth century, the earlier, sixteenth-century form being *fall of the leaf*).

Evening replaces an earlier *even* in late Middle English, but in large areas of the country, the word is simply not used in dialect, notably in the North of England and the South Midlands, and in isolated areas elsewhere, for example, the informants at Steeple Ashton and Netheravon expressly stated that *evening* was not used – a reminder of the importance of negative evidence.

(H)ook (see OED under *holk* and D&G under *uck*) meaning to *root up*, in its present distribution centred on Wiltshire and its immediate borders to the east, and found otherwise only in Northern England and Scotland is a venerable word reaching back to the fourteenth century, but is no longer found in the standard language.[50]

Two bodily ailments next; *dandruff* and the *tremors*. *Scurf* is widespread in dialect and was the standard word from late Old English times, being eclipsed by *dandruff* only in the sixteenth century. The use of the same word for *hangnail*, at Sutton Veny, shows semantic consistency, both afflictions having to do with loose scraps of skin. "Old people often can't keep their heads still; what would you say the trouble was?" asked SED. The responses, *nerves*, *trembles* and *shakes*, are all self-explanatory, but two others deserve further investigation: *shiggles* is probably not simply a variant of *jiggles*, for OED gives *shig* as meaning *shake* in a text of 1440, though not again until a glossary of Norfolk dialect published in 1893. *Shig* is thought to be derived from *shog*, and interestingly D&G record that verb in the sense, "to sift ashes etc. by *shaking* the sieve". *(The) fifer's dance* from Burbage is an amusing folk-etymological corruption of *St. Vitus's dance*, as if it were a dance to the music of the fife!

For the last lexical investigation, let us look at a word not recorded by SED, nor heard by D&G, nor, strangely, given an entry in OED, and certainly obsolete by now, though it may have lasted into the eighteenth century. Aubrey records it in his *Remaines of Gentilisme and Judaisme* as follows: "The Shepheards, and vulgar people in South Wilts call Februarie Sowlegrove: and have this proverbe of it: viz Sowlegrove sil lew. February is seldome warme." (*Lew* was heard by D&G, and survives, incidentally, as the first element of StE *luke*warm.)

D&G venture no etymology of *Sowlegrove*, but there are several pieces of evidence that can help elucidate the problem: even before Aubrey's time, as far back as the mid-sixteenth century, February was also known as 'February Fill-dyke', and Richard Jefferies also notes this as current in Wiltshire in his day: "February 'fill ditch', as the old folk call it, on account of the rains". The eighth century Anglo-Saxon scholar, Bede, in his work on chronology, *De temporum ratione*[51] writes, "February was called *Solmōnath* (i.e. "Solmonth") in heathen times", which seems to suggest that we are dealing with the same first element at least. Under *sole*[52] OED records an eighteenth century Kentish dialect word meaning *pond, pool*, or, in the words of the 1736 citation, "a dirty pond of standing water" – the word is derived from OE *sol*, meaning *mire, miry or muddy place*, and EPNE lists it as "fairly common in Old English charters". In the sense, *miry pool*, it is probably – according to the editors of PNW (340) – the origin of *Soley*, near Chilton Foliat (spelt *Sowley* in 1619) and of the derived surname, *Sole*.[53] In view of "February Fill-dyke", it is then difficult not to take *-grove* as deriving from OE *græf* or **grafa*, a *trench, ditch*.[54] On this presentation of the evidence, then, *sowlegrove* is interpreted as a native English epithet of the month February, closely parallel in meaning to *Fill-dyke*, and itself meaning something like *miry/muddy ditch*.

NOTES

1 An example, incidentally, of "false division" or metanalysis; others are: *an orange, an apron, an umpire*, which should "correctly" be **a norange, *a napron, *a numpire*; compare note 3 below.

2 Though the noun, *vomit*, is found from the late fourteenth century onwards.

3 The same process as is illustrated in note 1 above, but in reverse: *a newt* should "correctly" be *an ewt*, and *a nickname*, *an ickname*.

4 See OED under *eaves* citing Elworthy, F. T. 1886. *The West Somerset word book*.

5 See, for example, Smith, A. H. 1956. *English place-name elements* (EPNE).

6 See WGE Map 33. Botanically the situation is complicated by the interchange of the names *whin, gorse* and *furze*. All three are used for *Ulex europaeus* whereas for the dwarf species *Ulex minor*, dwarf *furze* or petty *whin* are commonly used. True *whins* belong to the genus *Genista* of which several species occur in Britain, but only one, *Genista anglica* is colloquially known as *whin*, the others being generally called *greenweeds*.

7 Note the adjectival *-en* termination, as discussed in Chapter 3: Adjectives: Types of Formation.

8 Compare also the compound *grass-ground* recorded by OED under *grass* sb.[1] 12a., but only from seventeenth and eighteenth century citations. The word was, however, transplanted to Newfoundland, see DNE under *grass-ground*.

9 See Fischer, A. 1976. *op.cit.* 109.

10 Found, for example, in children's stories featuring Brock the Badger.

11 Wakelin, M. F. 1970. "Welsh influence in the West of England: dialectal 'Tallet'." *Folk life* 8: 72–80.

12 Recorded only once by SED from Ashton Keynes, in the form, *emmetumps* – it must, however, be admitted, that this could be analysed as *emmet-(h)umps*, with dropped *h*; there is, however, the supporting evidence of *wanty-tump* in D&G's 1934 Addenda. In the same Addenda, D&G note an interesting word for *ant-hill*, i.e. *emmet-but*, also recorded throughout Dorset by SED. (See further OED under *butt* sb.[5]) D&G also note *emmet-knoll* in their 1899 Addenda.

13 Note also, Buttington *Tump*, and Hetty Pegler's *Tump*, both in Gloucestershire. OED notes that the Welsh word *twmpath* means, "a clump or tuft of rough grass, a barrow or tumulus", and that it is found in the Middle Welsh *Mabinogion*, with which form, compare *tumpet*, recorded in EDD. The Latin *tumulus* is possibly cognate.

14 See *Geiriadur Prifysgol Cymru* (*University of Wales dictionary*) under *cam*.

15 We prefer, in spite of Fischer, A. 1976. *op. cit.* 76 & 157, to relate *gammy* to *cam* via the Welsh *c: g* initial mutation pattern. (Compare the remark at *kex* in Chapter 6.) It should, however, be noted that the adjective *gammy* is almost always restricted to qualifying *leg*, and that

the most probable etymology, therefore, is perhaps one that sees a relation with French *jambe*, Italian *gamba*, etc. (compare also, the Wiltshire dialect word *gambrel* used in the Wiltshire dialect antimasque of 1636). An intriguing alternative is Brian Cleeve's suggestion (*A view of the Irish*, 1983: 180) that the word derives from Sheldru, the language of the Irish tinkers, where the term *g'ami* means *bad*.

16 See OED under *thwart*. This seems a preferable explanation to that offered by Fischer, A. 1976. *op. cit.* 93–4.

17 The obvious and most plausible origin for this word is to see it as an adjectival derivative in *-(e)n* of the OE *duru*, ancestor of our Modern English *door*, with the normal mutation of the root-vowel. A good parallel is OE *byrgen* from *burg*, as in the Yorkshire place-name, *Burn*.

18 For an extended discussion of this, see Fischer, A. 1976. *op. cit.* 111–123.

19 Fischer, A. 1976. *op. cit.* 268 suggests a blend of *darling* and *doll*. cf. Hewins, G. 1981. *The Dillen*.

20 See DNE under *nuzzle-tripe*, and compare the obsolete *nestle-cock*, the last-hatched or weakling of a brood of birds (OED); SED also records *nestle-bird* for runt, from Cornwall and Devon. The first element is usually taken to be the common verb, *nestle* (could this be the origin of *nisgal*?); the second is taken by the editors of WGE to be *tripe* in the colloquial sense, *rubbish* (compare the Cornwall and Devon *-draff* forms, which also mean *refuse, dregs; -dredge*, also from Devon, is probably a form of *dreg(s)*), though we might perhaps suspect that *trip*, a collective term for a *litter of piglets* (recorded by SED from Sutton Veny and Fovant), could also be involved. Note that D&G in their 1899 Addenda record *trip* as a verb used in north Wiltshire meaning (of a sow) *to give birth*. In Lydgate (*a*.1410) *The Churl and the Bird* there is a reference to, "... rude swyn, that love draff of kynde".

21 See DHS.

22 According to Dyer, T. F. 1878. *English folk-lore*: 115, "To meet with a shrew-mouse in going a journey is said, by the Northamptonshire peasantry, to be unlucky." There is possibly an instance of a shepherd protecting his sheep from the path of two shrews (described as *all-wyghtys* – glossed as "uncanny creatures") by turning his flock around, in the second Wakefield Shepherds Play (lines 35ff), of 1400X1450. See Malone, K. 1925. "A note on the Towneley *Secunda pastorum*," *Modern language notes*, 40: 35–9. We now make a distinction between shrews, which are insectivores, and mice, which are rodents. There are three British mainland species of shrew: the common shrew, *Sorex araneus*; pygmy shrew, *Sorex minutus*; and water shrew, *Neomys fodiens*.

23 This probably bears the same phonological relationship to *flitch* as

hack to *hatch*, etc. See further examples listed in Chapter 7, note 24.

24 The form, *(h)enge*, of this word, which is etymologically related to the verb, *hang,* because the organs "hang" in the body of the animal, should be compared with the place-name element, *henge,* originating in our county's *Stonehenge,* and derived from OE *hengen, gallows, gibbet,* which also implies the idea of hanging.

25 Mabbs, A. W. (ed.) 1953. *Guild stewards' book of the Borough of Calne, 1561–1688* (Wiltshire Record Society, volume 7). See further the remark on the place-name *Red Shore* in Chapter 5.

26 See PNW: 34.

27 See PNW: 319. Note also the disguised *Shippen* field name, *Sheephouse Close*, in North Newnton (*Shippingclose* in 1570) cited in Field, J. 1972. *English field names: a dictionary.*

28 The same seems likely to have happened to *bull-beggar* (see OED).

29 For an interesting discussion of *bogey* and related words see Widdowson, J. 1971. *Folklore* 82: 99–115.

30 *Hodmandod* sense 3.

31 Varia XVI.

32 *Hodmandod* sense 1.

33 This should go some way towards explaining the difficulty acknowledged by Fischer, A. 1976. *op. cit.* 223.

34 See D&G under *hyle* and OED under *hill* v^2.

35 See D&G under *mow* and OED under *mow* sb.^{1} sense 2.

36 Fischer, A. 1976. *op. cit.* 144–6 seems to have missed these forms in his discussion.

37 Farr, M.W. 1959. *Accounts and surveys of the Wiltshire lands of Adam de Stratton, 1268–86* (Wiltshire Record Society, volume 14).

38 OED *Feign* v. sense 13.

39 *Fainites* is a corruption of *Feign I* v.OED.

40 See also Clark, A. L. 1893–4. "Wiltshire children's games", *Wiltshire notes and queries* 1:160–4, 200–6 and Tanner, H. and Tanner, R. 1939. *Wiltshire village* which includes a remarkable collection of children's rhyming and counting games.

41 See EDD under *clitch*^{2}.

42 See OED under *keck*, meaning *retch*.

43 Now to be found in the 1972 *Supplement* under *dunny* sb^2.

44 See further *dain* in Chapter 6.

45 Under *Fresh* sense 4b.

46 For example, see D&G under *scram, stiff as if benumbed; scrump* in its three senses: *a very dried-up bit of anything,* hence, *a shrivelled-up old man,* and *screw-up (one's face)*; and *shrump up, hunch up the shoulders.*

47 For the semantics we must remember that toilet paper is a very recent

introduction, compare the Arab taboo against using the left hand for the same reason. "In many cultures the left hand is regarded as the 'unclean' hand, used for sexual and excretory purposes" (Hertz, R. 1973. "The pre-eminence of the right hand; a study in religious polarity" in Needham, R. (ed.) *Right and left, essays on dual symbolic classification*.

48 Is there conceivably a connection with *Wat*, one of the names used for hare?

49 Grigson, G. 1958. *The Englishman's flora*, 368–9.

50 See Glausser, B. 1974. *The Scottish–English linguistic border: lexical aspects*.

51 See Jones, C. W. 1943. *Opera de temporibus*, chapter 15.

52 i.e. *sole* sb[4].

53 See Reaney, P. H. 1967. *The origin of English surnames*, 51; 352.

54 These forms would normally be expected to develop into modern -*grave*, but it is precisely in our county that the editor of ODEPN has suggested the selfsame anomalous development in the place-name *Grovely (Wood)*; what makes it unlikely that the first element is OE *grāfe* or *grǣfe*, a *grove, copse*, despite the fact that this is a forest name, is that this meaning is probably already present in the second element, *leah*, meaning a *wood*, and further, that as he remarks, "Through Grovely Wood runs a Roman Road, called on the map 'Ditch' part of the way. This might have been called *grafa*". (The ditch and the Roman road are in fact distinct, but adjacent, archaeological features.)

5

Specialised Lexicon: Place-Names and Surnames[1]

PLACE-NAMES

Introduction

"... In the late Middle English period [dominant dialects, such as Central Midland] became the prevailing written forms in their own times, and so usually the reflection of genuine local speech in the literature and written documents of other areas tends to disappear. Most place-names, however, at least until the sixteenth century, adhere much more closely to local patterns of speech" (EPNE: xxix).

Phonology

All the changes we have discussed in Chapter 2 with regard to the general lexicon can also be observed in Wiltshire place-names, often with valuable evidence that helps to date these changes, for example:

INITIAL CONSONANTS

f *appearing initially as* v:

The very early (late eleventh century) example of *Viteletone*, *Fittleton*, has already been considered. Other early instances: (*East*) *Foscote* (near Grittleton) contains OE *fox*, a *fox*, as its first element; *c.*1250, this appears in a document spelt *Voxcote*, though later forms and the present spelling have "corrected" this earlier pronunciation; compare *Vaux* Hill field (West Lavington) which does retain the earlier

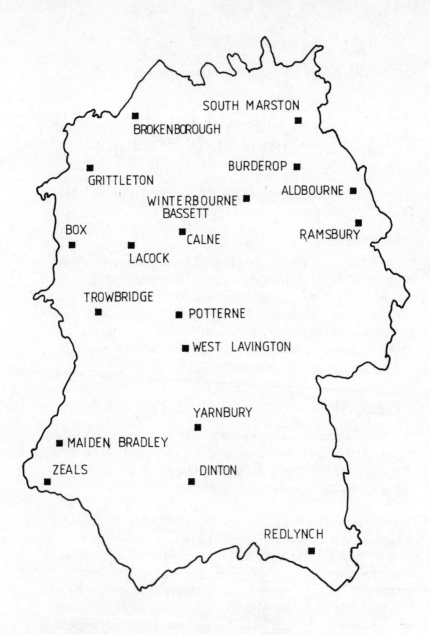

18 *Some principal Wiltshire place locations mentioned in Chapter 5.*

South-Western pronunciation of *fox*. *Sutton Veny* (pronounced "venny"), earlier Veny Sutton, is spelt *Fenni*sutton in thirteenth century documents, and was called *fenny*, on account of its marshy situation. (Compare in other parts of the country the non-South-Western form: *Feni*scowles (Lancashire); *Fenny*mere (Shropshire); and *Fenny* Bentley (Derbyshire), *Fenny* Compton (Warwickshire) and *Fenny* Drayton (Leicestershire).) Occasionally what may be examples of hypercorrection can be found, as in Stoke *F*arthing, which was quite rightly spelled Stoke *V*erdon by Aubrey in the late seventeenth century (in his remarks on the dwarf-elder cited in Chapter 6) as it belonged to John de Verdun in the thirteenth century, originally from Verdun in France. The second element in the name has first been "corrected" to *F*erdon, and then folk-etymologised to *F*arthing.

s appearing initially as z:
The most notable example is *Zeals* (though the earliest example spelt with *z*- is late (1637)), from OE *sealh*, *willow*, (Modern English *sally*) especially when we consider *Selwood*, which contains the same element. On Andrew's and Dury's *Map of Wiltshire* of 1773, *Zons Barns* appears on the site of the modern *Sands' Farm* (Donhead St. Andrew).

thr appearing as dr:
Drock Piece (Winterbourne Bassett) contains the dialect word, *drock*, a common element in Wiltshire field-names, meaning *a covered drain*, from OE *throc* (see D&G under *drock* and EPNE under *throc*). Note, too, Hill*drop*, near Ramsbury, and Bur*derop* (pronounced "*Bur-drop*") where the second element is from OE *throp*, *hamlet*.

VOWELS
e sound before -dge, -g *(and*-sh*) appearing as* ai *sound*:
Perhaps to be found (formerly, at least, if no longer) in Swatn*age* Wood, Charlton, near Malmesbury – if pro-

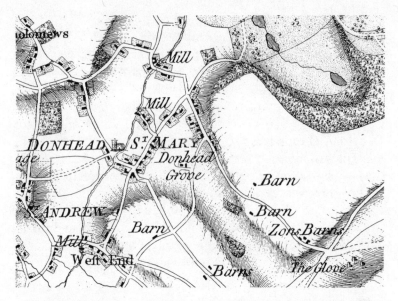

19 *Enlarged portion of Andrews and Dury's* Map of Wiltshire, *1773, showing Zons Barn on the site of the modern Sand's Farm, Donhead St. Andrew.*

nounced as in StE "age" – where the second element is derived from *hedge*.

a *sound before* -sh *also appearing as* ai *sound*:
Naishes Farm (Compton Chamberlayne), and *Naishe* House, near Bremhill, are both from ME atten *ashe*, *at the ash-tree*, showing the common Middle English false division of the phrase in such a context. (For the phonology compare *ash* mentioned above.)

SEMI-VOWELS
Loss of initial w:
Woodhill Park near Clyffe Pypard, a name compounded from OE *wād*, *woad*, plus *hyll*, *hill*, was formerly pronounced *Oadle* Park, and appears thus spelt on an 1820 map of Wiltshire, and as *Odehill* in a document dated as early as 1497.

addition of w:

This feature can be seen in Brick*worth* House, near White-parish, where the second element is OE *ōra*, *slope*, *bank* (compare the 1561 spelling, Brec*orr*); this is a common element in field-names where the field is bounded by a stream, compare *War* Field (Lyneham); *Whyr* Fields (Avebury) and those mentioned at PNW:442.

Loss of initial y:

Yatton Keynell, with original initial *y* sound, was also known as *Eaton* Keynell in the seventeenth century.

Addition of y:

Possible examples of the addition of *y* initially are *Y*arnfield (near Maiden Bradley), and *Y*arnbury Castle (near the Langfords), if their first element is, indeed, as PNW is prepared to allow, OE *earn*, *eagle* (archaic *erne*). PNW gives both Castle and Water *Eaton* (from original OE *ēa* plus *tun*) as formerly pronounced "*Yetn*" (and found spelt *Yetton* in 1442 and 1553). *Yea* Mead, a field lying by the Avon in Bradford-on-Avon, contains the same OE element, *ēa*, *water*. Incidentally, the surname *Yeo* (and *Atyeo*) is derived from this same dialect development of the place-name.

OTHER CHANGES INVOLVING THE SOUNDS
REPRESENTED BY THE LETTERS *h* AND *r*
treatment of the initial h

Clatt*ingar* near Oaksey, contains OE *hangra*, SW *hanger* (discussed below), as its second element. The opposite feature, hypercorrection, is shown for this sound in *Hinnocks*, the local pronunciation of *Ennox* (Wood) near Box, from the ME element *inhok*, treated below.

treatment of r

There are at least two examples of metathesis involving *r* in PNW, both in field-names; the only enduring instance being

Stricklease (Lacock), probably from OE *stirc*, dialect *stirk*, a young heifer.

Some place-name elements (mainly south-western)

We have already noted several place-name elements in passing in the general discussion of the dialect lexicon, for example, *ground* and *gorse*. Some other elements were elicited by the SED survey, for example, "What do you call that low-lying flat land in the bend of a river, generally very fertile?" *(H)ams* was the response from Ashton Keynes and Sutton Veny; this is the OE element *hamm*, as in Damerham, Grittenham, Chippenham and Inglesham, etc., not always easily separated from the similar-looking OE *ham*, *village*, *homestead*.

Here is what the place-name scholar, Margaret Gelling, has to say about the element OE *beorg*, *barrow*, *burial mound*: "The adoption of this word by modern archaeologists as a technical term for a tumulus was due to its survival in that sense in the dialect speech of Wessex and the south-west, an area which attracted much early archaeological attention" (*Signposts to the past* (1978): 132). She goes on to quote the OED's first modern citation for this sense from Lambarde's *Perambulation of Kent* (1576): "These hillocks, in the West Countrie (where is no small store of the like) are called Barowes ... which signifieth sepulchres". OED's next citation is also of interest (1656): "Those round hills, which in the Plains of Wiltshire are ... by the Inhabitants termed Barrowes..." The editors of PNW note: "We have several examples of *beorh dūn* bringing before us a typical Wiltshire landscape – a barrow-strewn down". The Wiltshire place-name *Brokenborough* is likely to refer to a barrow which was plundered already in antiquity. The hundred name, *Rowborough*, and the farm of that name in South Marston may also refer to raided barrows[2]; as we saw in Swan*borough* Tump, the site of an ancient barrow was often chosen in Anglo-Saxon times as the meeting-place of the hundred (compare *Barrow Hundred*, Dorset, formerly *Hundredesberewe*.)

20   *Barrow-strewn Wiltshire landscape, an engraving by Philip Crocker for Sir Richard Colt Hoare's* Ancient Wiltshire, *vol. 2, 1821.*

The Wiltshire Downs have always been prime sheep-grazing land, and in the names of *Sleight* Farm (Potterne), and *Sleight* House (Winkfield),[3] is preserved the South-West dialect *sleight, a sheep pasture* (from OE **slæget, *sleget*). (D&G cite Davis's *General view of the agriculture of Wiltshire* (1794); OED's first citation is from Aubrey *c.*1670 in the form *slaights*. EPNE notes the dialect spelling *slait*.)

Snapes (near Dinton), and *Snap* (Aldbourne), and South-West dialect *snap, snape*, derive from OE *snæp, boggy land*. (The latter place lies in a bottom at the foot of the chalk downs.) Other more generally distributed English dialect words for *bog(gy land)* found in Wiltshire include: *quob*, found in the names *Quob*well Farm (near Malmesbury), and *Quobbs* Farm (near Calne). The *Gog* (near Allington) is by a small stream; compare Aubrey in his *Natural history of Wiltshire* – "In Minety Common in Bradon Forest, neer the rode

87

which leadeth to Ashton Caynes, is a boggy place called the Gogges, where is a spring, or springs, rising up out of fuller's earth." The low-lying *Sunt* Copse (near Redlynch) preserves an Old English word related to *swamp* and *sump*. *Stroud* Farm (Lacock and Rowde), and *Stroud* Hill Farm (Potterne), derive from OE *strōd*, *marsh*.

Other elements found only in South-Western place-names include *splot-* (PNW); for example, The *Splatts* (near Heddington) – *a patch of land*; a South-West word surviving in Gloucestershire dialect as *fellet*, *a portion of wood felled annually*, occurs with the meaning *clump of felled trees, place cleared by felling*, as the first element of the field-name, *Felt*-ham (Edington); *Sprays* Farm (near Calne), and Ham*spray* House (at Ham), derive from OE *spræg*, *brushwood*, preserved in this sense in South-Western dialect, compare Hardy's *Woodlanders*: "All he had required had been a few bundles of spray for his man Robert". (StE *spray* (of cut flowers) is the same word, but not found in this sense till the nineteenth century); *Ennox* Wood (near Box), usually pronounced *Hinnocks*, *Ennix* Wood (near Bremhill), and *Innox* Mill (Trowbridge), are from ME *inhok* (the final -*x* represents -*ks*), while the many fields named *Hitching* or similar (compare *Hitchen* Copse, Chilton Foliat) are from the related ME *hecchinge* (compare also ME *inheche*), and both sets of names seem to reflect a South-Western agricultural practice in which the most productive piece of land (for example, in a common field) was temporarily enclosed for cultivation during such time as the rest of the surrounding land was allowed to lie fallow: D&G give *Hookland* (or *Hitchland*) Field from Davis[4] but also add "Parts of some fields are still [i.e. *c*.1890] known as *Hooklands* in South Wiltshire, though the system has died out."

Cleeve was offered in response to SED for a (steep) *slope* at Netheravon (compare *Cleve Hill*, Newton Tony, and others near West Knoyle, and Charlton near Upavon; *The Cleeve* near Corsham, and another near Orcheston St. George; *Cleeve Hill House*, Limpley Stoke, etc.); the word is closely related to StE *cliff* (being simply an oblique case), but as a simple noun (rather than a place-name element), it now seems to be restricted to South-Western dialect, and Somerset in particular.[5]

Ant- and *mole-hills* are known in parts of the county as *emmet-* and (*want*)-*molds* (compare -*moles* in the West Midlands). *Mould* survives in the standard language as a somewhat archaic word for *topsoil, earth*, and OED notes that the plural, *moulds*, in dialect only, can mean *lumps or clods of earth*, so that it might be thought that *ant-/mole-hill* would be a natural extension of meaning; it should be noted, however, that from Sutton Veny, *mow*, meaning a *slope* was recorded, as well as the expression, *on the mow* for *sloping* (this is the same word as that discussed above in the sense *hayloft* and earlier, *haystack*, from Burbage, see D&G under *mow* & *wind mow*). In the sense *slope*, it is a remarkable survival of OED's sense, "A heap or pile; also, a heap of earth, a mound, a hillock", attested from the fifteenth century, but not beyond 1681. In this sense, the word is also a place-name element (see EPNE under *mūga*) as in *Mow Cop* (Cheshire), "a hill, on a boundary, perhaps referring to a boundary cairn", and the hundred name, *Lamua*, in neighbouring Berkshire (prefaced by the French definite article) meaning "probably, a mound where the hundred met." Given, then, the undoubted survival of this word, it may well be – considering its more precisely appropriate meaning *heap of earth, mound, hillock* – that in reality it is *mow* rather than *mould* that is the second element of *emmet-/want-mold* with inorganic *d*, or that it has been folk-etymologised to -*mold*, either because of the appropriateness of *mould*, or because of contamination by the word *mole/mold* (i.e. StE *mole*. *Mold* appears as a Wiltshire dialect variant of StE *mole* at Sutton Veny and Whiteparish).

A case study in onomastics

Now a look at the sort of dialect information to be gleaned

from large scale maps (the study of place-names in this context is known as ONOMASTICS); the best examples are the Tithe Award maps of *c*.1840 held in the County Record Office. The following names are drawn from two large-scale maps covering the Alton Barnes, Alton Priors and Woodborough area. We begin with a consideration of the Altons map: the fields either side of the Wansdyke are called *Long Barton* and *Holly Bush Barton*, featuring the word *barton* which we have already discussed. There is a gap in the Wansdyke where the prehistoric Ridgeway path crosses it labelled "*Red Shore*"; in 1570 this was spelt *Reddscherd*, and can thus be seen to contain the dialect word, *shard*, *gap (in a hedge)*, also discussed elsewhere; compare White*shard* Bottom near Mildenhall, another gap in another dyke. *Red* refers to the colour of the dyke's soil as revealed by the gap (PNW). A field called *The Hanging*, i.e. a hillside field (D&G under *hanging*), may be compared with *Hanging* Langford, so called "from its position below a steep hillside" (PNW). (Compare the common field-name element, *-hanger*, *a slope*, later, *a wooded slope*: PNW under *hangra* lists eight major names also employing this element.) The group of fields between the Wansdyke and White Horse Hill all contain the South-Western dialect word, *bake*, for example North *Bake*, *Bake* Penning, etc., earlier *beak*, meaning "land reclaimed for ploughing by clearing it with a mattock and burning the rubbish".[6]

According to the editors of PNW, *Golden Ball Hill* was so-called from a Wiltshire dialect name for the *rockrose* (*Helianthemum*), with its brilliant yellow flowers which covered the hill-top. However, Grose, in his *Flora of Wiltshire* (1957), writes:

Several weeks ... before the rockrose is in bloom, the rounded slopes are yellow with cowslips and later in the season with birds-foot trefoil and horseshoe vetch. When these fade the yellow coloration is succeeded by a beautiful golden brown, a wonderful sight as illuminated by the setting sun and seen from the Vale of Pewsey.

It is due, surprisingly, to the innumerable flower-heads of salad burnet, so sombre and yet so resplendent en masse, which does have a ball-flower.

Both authorities appear to interpret the name in terms of the shape and colour of individual plants rather than in terms of the overall topography of the hill itself which has a distinctive ball-shape, especially when accentuated by the yellow hue imparted by various spring flowers.[7]

The neighbouring *Knap* Hill shows the fairly common word, *knap*, *a little hill*; *a steep ascent in a road* (D&G citing Slow's Glossary), PNW lists seven other major names employing this word. On top of Knap Hill there is a well-known pre-historic earth*work*, and it is on account of this that the long narrow field to the south of the hill is called *Workway*, not as one might quite naturally have thought, from a track taking farm labourers to work – such are the dangers of folk-etymology!

One could almost have written "pitfalls", for on the Woodborough Parish map are three fields named *Lambpit* Field, *Lambpit* Mead, and *Lambpit* Ground (so spelt, and, incidentally showing how the dialect is able to distinguish the three parts of what was probably originally one field, by means of its rich lexicon); a moment's reflection however impressed upon us the unlikelihood of *a pit for lambs! and, in fact, EPNE under OE *lām-pytt* informs us that "in Old English charters *lām-pytt*, *clay-pit*, is common", and lists *Lampitts* in Hertfordshire (compare *Lamb Pitts* and *Lampits* in Cheshire), and the less ambiguous *Loampit* in Surrey, of precisely the same derivation as our field-name. The field named *Pencil Veny* in the extreme south-east of the parish, close to its boundary, provides yet another lesson: at first, we assumed that this long, narrow field was called *Pencil* on account of its shape (a common enough procedure), and *Veny*, as in Sutton Veny, discussed above – mercifully, in a moment of sanity, it struck us that this was a folk-etymological spelling of *Pennsylvania*, a fairly common nick-

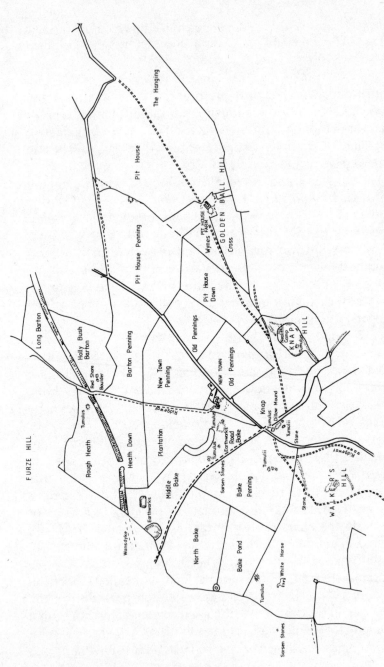

21 *Map of Alton Barnes and Alton Priors based on the 1838 tithe map for Alton Barnes and early Ordnance Survey mapping.*

92

name for a remote field! (PNW adds *Botany Bay, Jericho, New England, California, Quebec,* and *World's End* for similarly located fields.)[8]

There are many fields on the map called *Horse Leaze,* the meaning of which is pasture for horses. *Leaze* now restricted to dialect, preserves OE *læs, pasture, meadowland,* and is a common element in field-names.[9] The etymology offered by OED & ODEE is interesting: *læs* is said to be related to the root of OE *lætan, let,* and the original meaning of *leaze* would then have been *land let alone,* i.e. untilled, lying fallow. SED asked "What do you call land that you have ploughed but that you leave unsown for some time?" The response from Sutton Benger was *lea,* also from one location in Somerset, while in Cornwall the form *leaze* was actually recorded – all of which seems to provide confirmation of the suggested etymology. *Lea* was also recorded from the neighbouring counties of Somerset, Dorset and Hampshire in the sense *pasture* (i.e. the sense of *leaze* in the field-names under discussion) in response to the question, "What do you call the grassland where you graze cattle?" Compare OED's citation from Jefferies's *Hodge and his masters* (1880): "The dead, dry grass, and the innumerable tufts of the 'leaze' which the cattle have not eaten."[10]

Birds in Place-Names: The Implications for Landscape History

Of the ten charters accepted as genuine copies of documents issued by King Alfred of Wessex in the late ninth century, one, dated 892, contains a grant of land at North Newnton, near Pewsey, to ealdorman Æthelhelm.[11] The bounds of this estate, as set out in the charter, coincide with those of the present parish, and in Old English begin "be æfene stæthe on stintesford", that is, "along the Avon bank to the Stint's Ford". Simon Keynes, in the Penguin Classic edition of *Asser's life of King Alfred* (1983), has identified this no

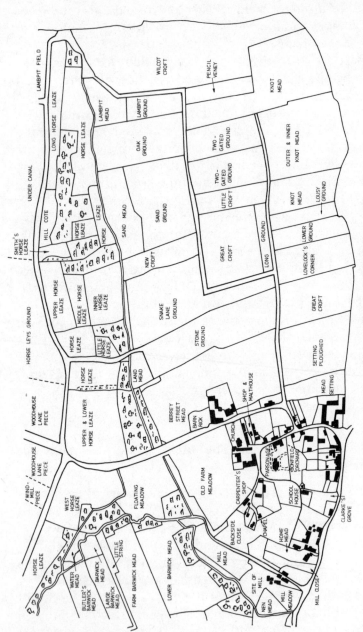

22 *A section of a parish map of Woodborough.*

longer extant place-name as being in the south-east corner of the parish at the point where the southern boundary meets the River Avon, i.e. at SU 136568. At present a line of fence posts continues the line of the Saxon boundary hedge down to the water.

23 *The hedgerow and fence demarcating the Saxon estate boundary at "Stintsford", North Newnton.*

But what of the first element in the ford-name? What is the meaning of *stint*? Dr. Keynes, in his interpretation of the charter, hesitantly suggests the meaning "ford where people were accustomed to take rest", i.e. Old English **stynt* (surviving in modern English *stint* as in "Don't *stint* yourselves!" and the derived *unstinting*). There was, however, another Old English **stint*, which does not turn up independently in the lexicographic record until the mid-fifteenth century,[12] but which has been deduced by scholars as the first element in the place-names *Stinchcombe* (Gloucestershire, earliest spelling *Stintescombe*) and *Stinsford* (Dorset), the latter identical to our name.[13] This is a bird name denoting in addition to the stints any of the smaller sandpipers, especially

95

the dunlin (OED), although this is not the modern usage.[14] There are plenty of parallel formations for such a ford haunted by the particular bird specified, for example, *Buntingford* (Hertfordshire), *Cranford* (Kent), *Gosford* (in seven different counties), *Ketford* (Gloucestershire, from the old English *cȳta*, *kite*) and another and nearby name from our own county, *Enford* (from the Old English *ened*, *duck*). In the light of this, Dr. Keynes, in a personal communication to the authors, has graciously conceded that our suggestion sounds "a good deal more plausible".

Stint, in this Old English usage, would be a vague term to denote any of the small waders. Strictly the Little Stint (*Calidris minuta*) occurs nowadays once or twice a year in ones and twos, due to the absence of any sizeable expanses of undisturbed water and thus water-edge and mudflat habitat. In the past, the Avon valley and other large river systems in the county had large associated tracts of marshland and, for part of the year at least, lagoons and mudbanks due to poor drainage. Small migratory waders may then have been commoner, and the dialect usage of *stint* may have referred to any or all of these. The habitat changes are corroborated by the historical and archaeological records.[15]

A similar historical change, but much less clear-cut in terms of species, in the avifauna of the county can be deduced from the place-name *Pickledean* near Marlborough. PNW records a sixteenth century spelling *Pykkeldean* but the earliest spelling is *Pytteldene* (the interchange of *t* and *k* was as common in Old English times as in more recent centuries, see remark under *Barton*). PNW and EPNE (under *pyttel*) interpret this name to mean "hawk-valley". OED (under *pittel*, *pitill*) records OE *bleri(a)-pittel* which is glossed *soricarius* which is itself elsewhere glossed as *mouse-hawk*. But we cannot now be certain which species of raptor was denoted by *pyttel* and, like *stint*, it may be a collective term referring to a number of different species; to this day certain downland valley sites attract migrant birds of prey and, at certain times of year, it is possible to observe several species on a single excursion.[16] *Pyttel* may also be like the related Old English bird name **puttoc* (and its root, **putta*, possibly to be found in the place-names, *Pitton* and *Puthall* (Farm), Little Bedwyn) which could include the *kite* and the *marsh harrier*, as it certainly did in the late nineteenth century: "It is said in Wiltshire that the *marsh harriers* or dun-pickles ... alight in great numbers on the downs before rain."[17] There is a similar uncertainty about which bird of prey is denoted by Old English *wrocc* found in our county as the first element of *Wraxall*.

SURNAMES

Just as with place-names, local surname forms – which are often derived from place-names, often, indeed, one and the same word – can also reveal features of South-Western dialect.

The surname *Hale(s)* derives from the OE place-name *halh* (the Anglian form), meaning *a (secluded) nook of land*, seen, for example, in places named *Hale(s)* in Norfolk, Shropshire, Staffordshire, and Worcestershire, all in that part of the country settled by Anglian rather than Saxon peoples, but the West Saxon form of the OE word was *healh*, and consequently the SW form of the surname is *Heal(es)*, *He(a)le*, and compare the place-names, *Heale* House (Woodford), and *Heal*, and *Hele*, in Devon. Similarly the Anglian OE *wella*, *well* gave rise to the places named *Well* in Lincolnshire and North Yorkshire, *Wellow*, Northamptonshire, and many of the numerous place-names ending in -*well*, and the derived surnames, *Wells* and *Atwell*; the adoption by StE of the Anglian form, *well*, has mostly swamped the West Saxon form *wi(e)lla* (hence the unexpected *Wells* in Somerset), but it survives occasionally, as in *Wilcot*, and in the derived surnames *Will* and *Atwill*.

Again, OE *y* became (broadly speaking) ME *i* in the East Midlands and the North Country, *e* in the South East, and *u* in the Central Midlands and the South West; consequently,

from OE *hrycg*, StE developed *ridge* from a (broadly) Northern form, the origin of the common place-name element
and the derived surname, *Ridge*; *rudge* is the SW dialect
form, however, and occurs in Wiltshire in *Rudge* (near Frox-
field), and *Rud*loe House (near Box), and in the derived surname, *Rudge*. Compare D&G under *rudge* "the space
between two furrows in a ploughed field", which they label
as both North and South Wiltshire. Compare *ridges*, in this
sense as recorded by SED: the pronunciation *rudges* was
only recorded from central Wiltshire (Burbage, Steeple
Ashton, and Netheravon). Most significantly, *ridge*, in other
senses – (of a haystack), and (of a house) – was pronounced
as in StE in these same localities, showing how the dialect
phonology has here been made to serve a semantic purpose.

Similarly, the same dialectal sound changes we have noted
in the place-name evidence naturally show up in surnames
dependent on these place-names, for example, with *(Sutton)
Veny*, corresponding to StE *fen(ny)*, compare the derived
surname, *Fenn*, SW *Venn*.

The three instances of the surname, *Voller*, from the Swin-
don area, listed in the telephone directory, represent the SW
variant of the common occupational surname, *Fuller*, i.e.
one who cleans and thickens (*fulls*) cloth by beating it in an
alkaline solution. In general, the distribution of the Middle
English name *Fuller* is Southern and Eastern – a different
occupational term, *Tucker*, being found in the South West
(note *Tuckerton* in Somerset, from ME *tukere*).

NOTES

1 Details throughout "Place-Name" section from PNW. See also,
though his evidence is drawn from Cornwall, Devon, Somerset and
Dorset, Matthews, W. 1939. "South Western dialect in the early
modern period", *Neophilologus* 24: 195–209. Details throughout "Surnames" section from Reaney, P. H. 1967. *The origin of English surnames.*

2 If OE *rūh* (Modern English *rough*) could indeed bear this sense, as
surmised by the PNW editors (see 423 under *beorg*).

3 Winkfield is now generally spelled Wingfield.
4 Davis, T. 1794. *General view of the agriculture of the county of Wiltshire.*
5 See further OED under *cleve* sb.[1] 3.
6 See PNW under *Burnbake* and EPNE under *beak, bake* and *bete*[2] (ME), modern dialect *beat* (see OED under *beat* sb.[3] and *beat* v.[2]), i.e. "rough sods hacked off the ground for burning in preparing land for cultivation." At the latter entry, EPNE notes: "the phonological connexion with *beak* is obscure", and yet this final *k* : *t* alternation is not uncommon in our own dialect, compare *bleak* for *bleat*, recorded by SED from Steeple Ashton, Fovant and Whiteparish, and, in medial position, *barken* as a variant of *barton*. The *k* form is probably the original in the word under discussion, compare OED under *beck* sb.[3], from OE *becca, a kind of mattock*, attested in late Old English and then not again until the nineteenth century dialect of Sussex. (Some of the intervening history of the word can, however, be traced in the Medieval Latin forms: *be(s)chia, besc(i)a* (thirteenth century), and *becka* (fourteenth century) cited in Latham, R. E. 1965 *Revised Medieval Latin word-list*, and in the late thirteenth century documents concerning the Wiltshire holdings of Adam de Stratton (Farr, M. W. 1959 *op. cit.*). Note further, East Anglian dialect *becket.*

In agricultural terms, the words refer to a system of downland reclamation known as "paring and burning", which led to the transformation of large areas of sheepwalk as early as the eighteenth century. This system of land management was not without its critics even then:

... the consequence must be that the roots which hold the land together and have been a century in forming, are destroyed all at once and it is the work of another century to get a sward equal to the former, as arable land is totally incapable of bearing crops after the first or second. This has been the case of thousands of acres of the best turf on the Wiltshire Downs. (Stone, T. 1800. *A review of the corrected agricultural survey of Lincolnshire.)*

Longer term arable cultivation was made more viable by the introduction of artificial fertilizers in the nineteenth century:

There is a lighter description of this soil generally termed 'beakland' or downland, and more of this kind has been brought into cultivation within these few years inasmuch as vast breadths of the downs are broken up every year, and not, as was formerly the case, crops of corn taken till, according to a quaint expression, 'an old corn would not produce a new one', and then laid down 'to rest'; but there is now a more regular system of culture by the use of artificial manures. (Little, E. "The farming of Wiltshire", *Journal of the Royal Agricultural Society* 1: 161–79.)

Buckman, J. 1865 ("Geology in the county of Wilts in reference to agriculture and rural economy", *Bath and West agricultural journal* 13: 3–28) observed of the downs:

The grass is here short, but mixed with thyme and many sweet upland herbs, which doubtless greatly contribute to the flavour of Southdown mutton. These districts, however, are daily being encroached upon for arable cultivation, as on the Downs around Avebury, Marlborough, and even on Salisbury Plain itself.

The arable monoculture apparent on the downs today is the latest phase of this process. Species-rich chalk grassland has declined to the extent that important remaining areas need Nature Reserve or Site of Special Scientific Interest status for protection.

7 Despite the fact that this site is now a National Nature Reserve, the species diversity has declined in recent decades and the descriptions given by both authorities may no longer be so appropriate.

8 For discussion of field-names in particular, see Field, J. 1972. *English field names: a dictionary*.

9 It is NOT etymologically connected with the word *lea*, used somewhat loosely in modern times to mean a *meadow*, deriving from OE *lēah*, whose original meaning was *wood, glade in a wood*, but via the latter meaning, and the similarity in sound in modern times, *leaze* was often mistakenly understood as the plural of *lea*.

10 Chapter 11 cited under *lease* sb.[1].

11 Sawyer, P. H. 1968. *Anglo-Saxon charters: an annotated list*. See No. 348 = BCS 567.

12 See OED under *stint* sb.[2].

13 See ODEPN under *Stinchcombe* and EPNE under **stint*.

14 The *little stint*, an occasional visitor to Wiltshire, and in appearance rather like a small *dunlin*, is one of the smallest waders.

15 In a specifically ornithological context, these have been reviewed by Perrins, C. M. 1966. 'Historical background' in Radford M. C. *The birds of Berkshire and Oxfordshire* and Fisher, J. 1966. *The Shell bird book*. There are implications for other marshland birds, not just waders; Perrins, for example, suggests that *cranes* probably bred until the sixteenth century (although some were undoubtedly held in captivity, see Yapp, W. B. 1982. *Archives of natural history* 10: 479–500) and *bittern* would have been relatively numerous.

16 In particular, the Berkshire/Lambourn/Marlborough Downs and the Salisbury Plain are noted for their migrant birds of prey. Writing in the *Guardian*, in February, 1969, of one such site, W. D. Campbell recounted the experience of an observer who, on a single outing, had seen *peregrine*, *merlin*, *buzzard* and *short-eared owl* as well as resident *kestrel* and *sparrowhawk*.

17 Swainson, J. 1873. *Weather folk lore* 2: 242 (cited in OED). This is a

well-attested habit of *marsh harriers*, *red kites* and some other birds of prey. However, although Swainson's citation is a nineteenth century one, the *marsh harrier* was but an occasional visitor to the county at that time, and it undoubtedly refers to a much earlier tradition. Smith (*Birds of Wiltshire*, 1887) notes that the species was formerly "not uncommon" in the county but he had heard of it "swarming" only in Egypt.

6
Specialised Lexicon:
Plant Names

INTRODUCTION

A great wealth of local names for wild plants is scattered throughout the pages of D&G, though it seems unlikely that many of them are any longer current. Many are of comparatively recent origin and are nationally recorded vernacular names.

RESPONSES TO THE SURVEY OF ENGLISH DIALECTS

SED, section 2 of book II, deals with "weeds",[1] but little of interest is to be gleaned from it: *clites* and *cliders* for StE *goosegrass*, we have examined; also *tump* in the sense, *tuft of coarse grass, tussock*. At Fovant, such tufts were called *bennets*, the same as StE *bent* (*grass*), see Jefferies in *Hodge and his masters*: "the lowly convolvulus grew thickly among the tall dusty bennets." Interestingly, this is a fairly common place-name element (OE *beonet*), especially in *Bentley* (the origin of the surname) of which we have an example in our county in *Bentley Wood* (West Dean) (from *beonet* + *lēah*, i.e. "clearing where bent-grass grows") as well as in *Bentham House*, Purton (PNW). The response at Steeple Ashton was *bullpoll* which can also be found in the works of Jefferies: "Some bulrushes and great bunches of bullpolls ... The bullpoll sends up tall slender stalks with graceful feathery heads."[2]

Withwine(d) for StE *bindweed* is universal in Wiltshire. *Bedwine(d)* is another dialect form for *bindweed* (as well as for *Old man's beard*, the *wild clematis*, in which sense D&G record it for S.Wiltshire), recorded for example, from neighbouring Hampshire (*bithwine* from Hatherden only one mile over the Wiltshire border, and a mere ten miles from Great Bedwyn) and the plant name has been suggested as the derivation of the place name, Great *Bedwyn* (see, for example, ODEPN). In the final chapter of W. H. Hudson's *A shepherd's life*, which mainly concerns the period of the latter half of the nineteenth century, *bithywind* is given as another form of the name applied to *Old man's beard*, and the identity of the "Old Man" is made plain by that other dialect name old Caleb recalls, *Devil's guts*: both this name and the *-wind* names refer to the twisting, climbing and pliant nature of these plants. The first element, *with-* preserves the word *withe* no longer current in modern English, meaning "a flexible twig, usually of willow, used for binding or tying", closely related to the widespread dialect name, *withy*, for the StE *willow tree* (found throughout Wiltshire). Geoffrey Grigson, in his fascinating book, *The Englishman's flora* (1958) gives the following additional Wiltshire names for the bindweed: *Granny's nightcap, kettle* (for ? *kirtle*) *smock,* and *willow-wind* (this last may be found in Jefferies's *Round about a great estate*; note how it appears to gloss the first element of *withwind* discussed above). He also gives *greybeard*, *honesty* (Aubrey calls it *maiden's honesty* in his *Natural history of Wiltshire*), *Daddy's whiskers*, and *skipping ropes* (according to D&G, the first two are found in North Wiltshire, and the second two in South Wiltshire).[3]

PHRASE-NAMES, MAINLY HUMOROUS

Hudson mentions tiled cottage roofs overgrown with the yellow *stonecrop* or *welcome-home-husband-though-never-so-drunk*; but Grigson thinks this is rather the name for the *wall-pepper* or *golden moss* (D&G record the name *creeping*

104

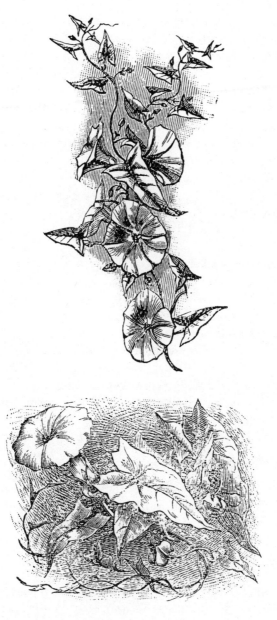

24 *Field bindweed (*Convolvulus arvensis*) and hedge bindweed*
(Calystegia sepium) *from F. E. Hulme's* Familiar wild flowers, *1877–1885.*

Jack for this plant from Lyneham. *Creeping Jenny* incidentally, denotes both *the ivy-leaved toadflax* and the *money-
wort*). A similarly extravagant name, *kiss-me-John-at-the-
garden-gate*, is given by Hudson for the *wild pansy*. *Loving
idols* and similar forms[4] are corruptions of the Elizabethan
name of this flower, *love-in-idleness*; these amorous associations are confirmed by the fact that it is the juice of this
flower that Oberon uses as a love-potion in Shakespeare's
Midsummer Night's Dream (note: in *Hamlet*, Shakespeare
has Ophelia refer to the flowers symbolically: "pansies,
that's for thoughts", showing his awareness of the word's
derivation from French *pensée, thought*).

FOLKLORE NAMES

Introduction

D&G derive many of their local names for plants (some of
which must no doubt have been *very* local) from the collec-
tions of Sunday-school-children inspired by a pastoral letter
from the Bishop of Salisbury in June 1889 (the names are to
be found in the *Salisbury Diocesan Gazette* from 1890), a
sample of these names follows together with some of their associated folklore.

Thunderflower

Thunder flower is a South Wiltshire name for the poppy
(*thunderbolt* is a Devon and West Country name, and Grigson cites others), due to a folklore belief that picking poppies
would call down thunder. Under *thunderflower*, OED
quotes Johnston's *"Flora Lindisfarniensis"* (1853): "About
Wooler it was wont to be called Thunderflower or Light-
nings, and children were afraid to pluck the flower, for if the
petals fell off the gatherer became more liable to be struck
with lightning." A correspondent to *Notes and queries*, 1880.
6th series, 2: 164; 273–4, reported overhearing a Stafford-

shire saying: "pluck poppies – make thunder," and this was also heard in Shropshire. (Other Wiltshire names from Grigson: *blindman* – D &G note that in Hamptworth it is "locally supposed to cause blindness, if looked at too long" – *redweed*, and *soldiers*, the last name doubtless harking back to the era of the red-coat.)

Snakeflower

Another plant with more than its fair share of folklore association is the *greater stitchwort* ("It is called in English Stitchwort, for its property in helping Stitches and pains in the sides" – Coles's *Adam in Eden: or nature's paradise* (1657). *Snakeflower* from Barford (compare *adder's meat* from Cornwall and neighbouring Somerset) is thus explained by Grigson: "Cornish children feared picking the flowers; if they did, the adder would bite them ... often in the spring, adders come out to sun themselves on the earthen hedges of the west country, which are whitened with Stitchwort.")[5] Names such as *snaps, snapjacks, pops, poppers* and, by confusion, *poppies* (also used of the foxglove for the same reason) and even the monstrous *Mother Shimbles snick needles* (the apparent proper name is probably a corruption of *thimble* – Grigson records *mother's thimble* also for Wiltshire) all allude to the "sounds which skilful fingers may elicit from the ripened seed vessels" (*Salisbury Diocesan Gazette*). Another children's game is alluded to in the name *fighting cocks* for the *spear* and other *plantains*, because, as D&G explain "Children 'fight' them, head against head".

Tom Thumb Names

At Zeals, the *bird's-foot trefoil* was known as *Tom Thumb's honeysuckles* and D&G also record the name *Tom Thumbs* from Mere, and Grigson lists over seventy other vernacular names for this plant including *Tom Thumb's fingers and thumbs* and *Hop-o'-my-thumb* from Somerset. Before Tom

107

Thumb became a nursery character, there is reason to believe he was a goblin (a common enough demotion), a small, active and no doubt mischievous one, along the lines of Robin Goodfellow or Puck, compare the Northamptonshire name for this plant, *Jack-jump-about*. (*Tommy Tottles* from Yorkshire, should perhaps be compared with the stories which feature a fairy named Tom Tit Tot or similar. Compare, for example, Rhys's *Celtic Folklore*: 548.) Other Wiltshire names given by Grigson record a perhaps deliberate Christianising of the flower, i.e. (Our) *Lady's fingers (and thumbs)*, (Our) *Lady's glove*, and (Our) *Lady's slipper*.

Witches

Thimbles (from Hamptworth – D&G) for the *harebell*[6] seems innocent enough, but reference to Grigson shows whose thimbles they were thought to be: a Somerset name was *witches' thimbles* (and we should remember that, according to widespread folklore belief, the hare is often a witch in animal form),[7] and two Celtic names translate as *goblin's thimble* (Ireland) and *fairies' thimble* (Isle of Man); compare the various *fairy* names from Dorset and Somerset, and the Wiltshire *fairy cap*. Elsewhere, however, the plant has saintly associations: St. George in other parts of the British Isles and St. Dominic in Roman Catholic countries.[8]

Divination

Now, two fascinating literary references to the practice of divination by flowers; the flower in this case being the *orpine*, known in Wiltshire as *midsummer-men*: John Aubrey, at the end of the seventeenth century reminisces:

I remember, the mayds (especially the Cooke mayds and Dayrymayds) would stick-up in some chinkes of the joists, etc., Midsummer-Men, which are slips of Orpins. They placed them by paires, sc: one for such a man, the other for such a mayd his sweet-

25 *Harebell (*Campanula rotundifolia*), associated with witches in Wiltshire and with saints elsewhere. (From F. E. Hulme's* Familiar wild flowers, *1877–1885.)*

heart, and accordingly as the Orpin did incline to, or recline from the other, that there would be love or aversion; if either did wither, death (*Remaines of Gentilisme and Judaisme* (1686–7)).

Two hundred years later, the Rev. Francis Kilvert, curate at Langley Burrell, noted in his diary entry for Wednesday, 11th June 1873: "In Gander Lane [Kington St. Michael] we saw in the banks some of the 'Midsummer Men' plants which my Mother remembers the servant maids and cottage girls sticking up in their houses and bedrooms on Midsummer Eve, for the purpose of divining about their sweethearts". Margaret Baker[9] notes that a correspondent in William Hone's *Table Book* (1827–8), who signed herself "Flower-bud" recorded the Sutton Benger form of this ritual: the girls picked two flowers (species not specified) which had not bloomed, pairing them to match the village sweethearts, tall or short, broad or thin. The initials of the couples were tied

26 *Orpine (Sedum* telephium*), divination species in Wiltshire. (From F. E. Hulme's* Familiar wild flowers, *1877–1885.)*

to the stamens and the flowers put into the hayloft in secrecy. If, after ten days, one flower had twined round another, a marriage was in store, but a turning away precursed a jilting. Early flowering meant early offspring, dead flowers a death to come, drooping portended sickness. "Their influence upon villagers is considerable", wrote Flowerbud. This folk-custom was taken to Newfoundland by immigrants from South-West England, and is recorded under *midsummer* in DNE thus: "if the two flowers (of *Midsummer Men*) grow together and intertwine it is true love between that couple. If, however, they grow apart the love will not last." There, however, the flower is identified as *rose-root* or (*yellow*) *stonecrop*; both are members of the same botanical *Sedum* genus as *orpine*.[10]

Danes' Blood

Danesblood is the colourful local name for the *dwarf elder*. Aubrey says of it: "about Slaughterford is plenty. There was heretofore a great fight with the Danes, which made the in-

110

habitants give it that name." This piece of folklore is very fully discussed in Grigson, and it seems, especially from the forms cited in the OED that, folk etymology has been at work in this name: the earlier name for the tree is *wallwort*, the form *Danewort* does not appear till the mid seventeenth century, but a century later the botanist, Parkinson, quoted in OED, wrote "It is supposed it took the name Danewort from the strong purging quality it hath, many times bringing them that use it into a flux [diarrhoea] which then we say they are troubled with the Danes". Interestingly, what must be the very same word has been noted as specifically a Wiltshire dialect word since the mid eighteenth century at least (Cunnington *MS.*, which defines it as "disagreeable effluvia – generally applied to those Scents which are supposed to convey infections") so there is probably no connexion with the Danes at all. A little later Aubrey adds "Dwarfe-elder at Box, &c, common enough: at Falston and Stoke Verdon,[11] in the high waies. The juice of ebulus turnes haire black; and being mingled with bull's fatt is Dr. Buller's remedie for the gowte" – a remnant of folk-medicine? In this connexion, incidentally, it is worth noting that the place name *Slaughterford* has nothing to do with *slaughter*, but is a development of OE *slāh-thorn*, i.e. *sloe-thorn/bush + ford*.

Although the form *Danewort* does not occur before the seventeenth century, J. Westwood has recently pointed out that *wallwort* as a name for dwarf elder has been associated with the Danes for at least a century before Camden's *Britannia* (1607). "In his account of the Danish conquest of Mercia, the historian John Rous of Warwick (d.1491) says that in villages where the people were slaughtered by the Danes one could see the herb *ebulus* still growing luxuriantly from the *ebullition* of their blood" (Westwood, J. 1985. *Albion: a guide to legendary Britain*: 104). More locally J. O. Halliwell, writing about 1800, reported: "When a schoolboy, I have often traced the intrenchments at Sherston Magna . . . and with other boys have gone in search of a certain plant in the field where the battle [of Sherston, between King Cnut and Edmund Ironside in 1016] was said to have been fought, which the inhabitants pretended dropt blood when gathered, and called *Danesblood* ... supposed to have sprung from the blood of the Danes slain in that battle" (Halliwell, J. O. 1849. *Popular rhymes and nursery tales of England*, cited by Westwood, *op. cit.*:61).

Other Names from Aubrey

Aubrey in the chapter entitled "Of Plants" of his *Natural history of Wiltshire* has the laconic note: "Naked-boys ... about Stocton" (near Wylye). He queries the identification himself, but *naked boys* is indeed a name for *meadow saffron*, the *autumn crocus* (also known in Wiltshire as the *Michaelmas crocus*), and another local name is *naked nanny* – it is so called, as D&G suggest, because the flower appears so naked without any leaves, which do not appear till the spring. At Maiden Bradley, Priory Farm includes the remains of a late twelfth century Augustinian Priory, once famous for its *saffron*, and the local school was able to add the minor name *Saffron Garden*, near the site of the Priory (PNW).

One last plant-name from Aubrey: *calver-keys*, one of the many plants he lists as growing near Easton Piercy, his birthplace. Grigson mentions earlier *culverkeys* recorded from Dorset and Somerset, despite the identification in OED as *columbine*, the common name attested as early as *c.*1300 deriving via Old French from Medieval Latin *columbina*, *dovelike*, containing *columba, dove. Culver* preserves the Old English *culfre, dove*, a much earlier borrowing from the Vulgar Latin diminutive of the word. (*Culver* appears also in Wiltshire place-names, especially minor and field names, for example *Culversleaze Copse*, Grafton, PNW.) The connexion is – as OED explains – "that the columbine's inverted flower has some resemblance to five doves clustered together". Other Wiltshire names listed by Grigson are *bachelor's/soldier's buttons, Cains and Abels, Granny-jump-*

112

out-of-bed and *Granny's nightcap*, also simply *nightcaps, Lady's slippers*, and *widow's weeds*.

USE-NAMES

Weatherglass

A plant old Caleb Bawcombe must have been familiar with was the *shepherd's weatherglass* or *scarlet pimpernel*, also known (at Barford) as the *ploughman's weatherglass*, or simply, throughout Wiltshire, as the *weatherglass*; this is because the flowers are sensitive to the temperature and humidity of the air, closing in wet or damp weather, and can thus be used as an indication of oncoming or continuing rain, a property alluded to by E. Darwin in his poem *The botanic garden* (1791):

> Closed is the pink-eyed Pimpernel;
> In fiery red the sun doth rise,
> Then wades through clouds to mount the skies;
> 'Twill surely rain – we see't with sorrow,
> No working in the fields to-morrow.

Clock Names

Next, two "clock" plants: *goat's-beard* or *Jack-go-to-bed-at-noon*, as it is in Wiltshire, whose flower, as the name suggests, closes at noon, and *star-of-Bethlehem* known in Wiltshire as *wake-at-noon* and *noon-peepers* (the latter attested by Grigson alone) whose flowers close early in the day and remain closed in dull weather. Again, there are poetic associations:

> And goodly now the noon-tide hour,
> When from his high meridian tower
> The sun looks down in majesty,
> What time about the grassy lea
> The Goat's Beard, prompt his rise to hail

113

With broad expanded disk, in veil
Close mantling wraps its yellow head
And goes, as peasants say, to bed.[12]

Comb and brush

Comb and brush interestingly seems to preserve something of the function implicit in the older and StE name for the plant, *teasel*, for in earlier times the spiky heads of these plants were used to *tease* out or separate the fibres of wool, etc., with a combing motion.

WILTSHIRE NAMES FOR PLANTS

A selection of names, made from D&G and the manuscript 'English plant names' by George Dartnell, held in the Library of the Wiltshire Archaeological & Natural History Society at Devizes, is given in Appendix 1. Scientific names have been revised where necessary and standardised on Rose's *The wild flower key* (1981). The names have been selected mainly because of their dialect or local interest but some nationally recorded vernacular names are included. Readers may like to try their hand at the etymology of some of the names for which we were unable to devote space for a detailed discussion in the text. The plant name enthusiast should consult the original sources; an indication of the extent to which a given name has a purely local distribution can be gained by cross-referencing with Grigson's *The Englishman's flora* (1957).

NOTES

1 Generally defined as a wild plant growing in a place where it is not wanted.
2 *Round about a great estate*, 1880, cited in OED. N.B. There is a botanical distinction between tussock *sedges* and *bulrushes*; the *sedges* are perennial grass-like herbs belonging to the family Cyperaceae, some of which form large, compact, tufts or tussocks around the margins of

114

wetland. The *bulrush* (*Scirpus lacustris*) is a particular species of sedge, frequently confused with the *common reedmace* (*Typha latifolia*) on account of the similarity of their flowering stems. Norman Rogers (pers.comm.) points out that *bennets* is also used in Wiltshire as a name for long, dry stems of grass.

3 Bindweeds belong to the Convolvulaceae family and the names here refer to the species *field bindweed* (*Convolvulus arvensis*) and the larger *hedge bindweed* (*Calystegia sepium*).

4 Wiltshire, K. 1975. *Wiltshire folklore*: 117, records the oral form, *love-a-li-dells*, an example of assimilation from the original *love-in-idleness* form.

5 See also Shakespeare's *Richard II* (III.ii.19–22): "And when they from thy bosom pluck a flower, Guard it, I pray thee, with a lurking adder, whose double tongue may with mortal touch, Throw death upon thy sovereign's enemies. This motif derives ultimately from the "snake-in-the-grass" proverb of Virgil's *Eclogue* III: 93. Perhaps it was the *stitchwort* that Shakespeare had in mind when he had Lady Macbeth advise her husband to "look like th' innocent flower, But be the serpent under it" (I.vi.67).

6 This is *Campanula rotundifolia*, one of the more widespread members of the bellflower family.

7 See for example "The Silver Sixpence" in Briggs, K. M. 1977. *British folk tales and legends: a sampler.*

8 Folkhard, R. 1892. *Plant lore, legends and lyrics.*

9 Baker, M. 1974. *The folklore and customs of love and marriage.*

10 The only other plant given the name *midsummer men*, according to Grigson's list, is *red valerian* in Somerset. On divination see also Drury, Susan M. 1986. "English love divinations using plants: an aspect," *Folklore* 97 (2): 210–214.

11 Falstone is Faulstone in Bishopstone (south Wiltshire); Stoke Verdon is Stoke Farthing in Broad Chalke.

12 Cited in Folkhard, R. 1892. *op. cit.*: 354.

7

Specialised Lexicon:
Bird Names

INTRODUCTION

There is a rich haul of Wiltshire bird-names scattered throughout the pages of D&G and other county sources, making up for very scant treatment in SED.[1] We propose to discuss only those names which are of interest mainly for their linguistic content, rather than as ornithological records.[2] However, in the case of some ecologically significant species, the historical context for the name may provide a perspective on the relationship between landscape change and species distribution which can be used to corroborate documentary evidence.

THE NAMES

Onomatopeic

OED marks *yaffingale*[3] (i.e. the *green woodpecker*) as South and South-West dialect, though it is not given by D&G, who instead note *yuckle*; in both words, however, the first syllables are supposed to be onomatopeic i.e. reproducing the cry of the bird. The considerable phonetic difference between the two attempts at rendering the woodpecker's cry, should teach us to tolerate a degree of latitude in this type of imitative formation.

There is far more agreement, however, and, indeed, we may feel, accuracy, in the various onomatopeic names for the *chaffinch*: firstly, the word *finch* itself is a development of a Primitive Germanic *fink which seems to have survived, alongside Old English *finc* (pronounced "*finch*"), into Middle English times, where it is preserved in the Hampshire place-name, *Finkley; pink* is the form preserved in the field-name, *Pinkham*, in Alvediston, and in *Pink Lane Farm*, Charlton near Malmesbury (PNW); the variants *tink* and *twink* are found in two other minor Wiltshire names, *Tinkmarsh* and *Twink Leaze* (PNW), D&G note *chink*, and finally there is the mainly Northern, Midland and East Anglian *spink*, not recorded from our county. (Welsh, too, has *gwinc* and *winc*.)[4]

Vocal Comparisons

These are not onomatopeic, in the sense that they do not "speak their own names", but are described in terms of their similarities with other sounds. *Johnny-/Jan-/Chan-chider*, for the *sedge warbler*, is a simple example, referring to the "chitter-chat" call of the bird.[5]

The *grasshopper warbler* is a shy, retiring bird which derives its standard name from the rapid, ticking call which it maintains for long periods and which is thought to resemble the chirping of the grasshopper. It is evident from the name *mowing-machine bird* recorded by D&G that the call resembles more the sound of early mechanical grass-cutters used for harvesting hay. Goddard himself wrote of the bird in his diary for 1881:

Hilmarton. April 11th 1881. This evening as it was getting dark I heard a noise just like the distant sound of a mowing machine, or the winding of a small clock wheel. It was near the front gate, but I made out with difficulty that it proceeded from the hedge on the other side of the road. Accordingly, I crept up near enough to see that it was a little sharp-beaked warbler about the shape and size of a Whitethroat, perhaps not so large, but I couldn't see distinctly as it was too dark. I have heard the sound many times here, but I could never find out where it came from before.[6]

Such a name is not necessarily of rustic origin – this style of local name may have arisen from the nineteenth century antiquarian tradition, of which Goddard was a part, in which case the origin is best described as intellectual.

27 *Grasshopper warbler, from Thomas Bewick's* A history of British birds, *1885 edition. It was known in Wiltshire at that time as* mowing-machine bird.

Behavioural Names

Many dialect names are behavioural, but others are based on some fancied resemblance, however, imaginative; an example of this latter type is *huckmuck* for the *long-tailed tit*. OED, citing fifteenth-century churchwardens' accounts from Yatton, Somerset, defines the word, with the help of Elworthy's late nineteenth-century *Somerset glossary*, as a special type of strainer used in brewing, made from an ovoid bundle of twigs. The connexion with the bird is the resemblance of its nest to a *huckmuck*: other names attested from

119

our county also alluding to the characteristic shape of the nest are *bottle tit* and *bombarrel tit*, the latter word is to be found in the seventeenth century form *bum-barrel*.[7]

Didapper, given by Maton as the Salisbury name for the *dabchick* or *little grebe*, is also of great antiquity, being a shortened form of *divedapper* found in Old English, and composed of the elements *dive* and *dop* (i.e. *dip*), alluding to its diving habit. D&G noted that the word was:

In common use in Salisbury until quite recently. Before the streams running through the city were covered over, it was an everyday occurrence to see a dripping urchin making for home, with an escort of friends at his heels yelling 'Diedapper, Diedapper, Diedapper, die!'.

Greenoak lists *scullery maids* as a Wiltshire name for the *pied wagtail*, and D&G give *(Polly) dishwasher*; both, she explains, arise from "the similarity between the constant up and down movement of the tails and the action of dipping and lifting made by a person washing or scrubbing clothes or dishes by the waterside." It is an old joke at the bird's expense; OED's first citation under *dishwasher* is from a book on hawking by the Dorsetshireman, Turbeville, printed in 1575: "The Wagtayles or dishwasher as we term them."

The widespread English name goatsucker for nightjar found from the seventeenth century is not of dialect origin but probably a learned translation from the Latin *Caprimulgus*. It is of interest, however, due to the bird's supposed habit of taking milk from goats and from cattle at night, which preserves the sort of primitive belief that, as Potter and Sargent surmise,[8] perhaps suggests a pastoral people observing the bird catching beetles and other insects which, at dusk, are attracted by the rank smell of goats. Indeed, *goatsucker*, is so prevalent in English literature, that other vernacular names, prior to the introduction of *nightjar* in the nineteenth century, must be regarded as provincialisms. The species has a rather specialised habitat – lowland heath, woodland with extensive glades and parkland – which limits its distribution, so that it is notable that in Wiltshire the name, *goat-sucker*, *is* reported from the Marlborough district, Savernake Forest being a probable stronghold of the species in the past.

Other behavioural and descriptive names recorded for Wiltshire include *thick-kneed bustard* for *stone curlew, rook hawk* for *hobby* and *nunny-fudger* for *wren. Thick-kneed bustard* has led to some confusion amongst ornithologists: Maton correctly pointed out that the *bustard* element refers to a very different genus, but W. H. Hudson, who was well

28 *Stone curlew from William Yarrell's* A history of British birds, *1843, formerly well known in Wiltshire as* thick-kneed bustard, great plover, Norfolk plover, pitch-penny *or* pitch-plug, *but now greatly reduced in number as a result of changes in downland agriculture.*

aware of standard nomenclature, used it in a purely descriptive, but nonetheless misleading, context:

The stone curlew, our little bustard with long wings, yellow eyes, and wild voice, still frequents the uncultivated downs, unhappily in diminishing numbers. (*A shepherd's life*, 1910)

The *thick-kneed* element is undoubtedly not of dialect origin (the "thickening" is not of sufficient magnitude to be noticed in casual observation) but a probable translation of the Latinised Greek *Oedicnemus*, used by the late eighteenth century systematists and subsequently by Maton. *Rook hawk* is rather obscure, but possibly refers to the breeding habit of the *hobby* which often takes over the deserted nest of a member of the crow family. At the same time as D&G were recording *nanny-* and *nunny-fudger* for the *wren,* the *Journal of American folklore* (cited in DNE) noted that in Newfoundland the word meant an *idler* or *shirker*! The word appears in EDD in the form *ninny-fudgy*.

Barley sower for the *common gull*,[9] heard in South Wiltshire in the 1850s (Smith), although not obviously dialect in its phonology as recorded (we should expect *zower*), is probably of rustic origin. In this context, *barley sower* may be regarded as a sobriquet or nickname;[10] it may also be fairly termed an *agricultural colloquialism*, as may *mowing-machine bird* for *grasshopper warbler*.

Place-Name Associations

Just as these agricultural colloquialisms may have an intellectual origin, a similar case can be made for the name *Beckhampton grey crow* for the *hooded crow*. This is a very local variant unknown to the contemporary Smith, for example, who lists the more widespread English place-name association, *Royston crow*, given for Wiltshire only by Im Thurn. It is not given by D&G although Goddard himself was aware of the variety, indeed, he was one of the last to record it as a regular winter visitor to Wiltshire:

Clyffe. November 27th 1884. There was a Hooded Crow about here all last winter (as he was the winter before). Sometimes he was with the Crows, sometimes with the Rooks, and now and then with the Jackdaws. I saw him continuously till about the end of February when he entirely disappeared and had not been seen since, until I saw him again at the beginning of this month.[11]

Thereafter, the bird became only an occasional visitor,[12] and the local name disappeared from use.

Commercial Colloquialisms

Three-pound-tenner might be termed a commercial colloquialism for the *goldfinch*, and derives from the social fashion of collecting in the Victorian period; it denotes a particularly large specimen with a high monetary value. A. P. Morres relates a conversation with a bird-catcher in the Salisbury district who used the term regularly.[13] About the year 1857, he trapped a white specimen of the larger sort which he sold for 5s.6d. Elsewhere in the county the large variety was known as the *chev(r)il*, but it seems the name is unlikely to refer to the villages named *Cheverell*[14] near Devizes (unless the collecting had been going much longer than has been thought). Colourful singing finches were widely exploited at this time: Im Thurn noted that goldfinch nests were seldom left undisturbed, the young invariably being taken for cage-birds, and the diary of another Wiltshire ornithologist, J. R. G. Gwatkin,[15] records that a chaffinch nest "beautifully studded with fragments from a pack of cards" sold for £30 around the turn of the nineteenth century at a time when £1 would have been a good weekly wage for a farm labourer.[16]

Hybrid Formations

The text of an Alton Barnes mummers' play reveals one of the protagonists to be called *"Turkey Snipe"*. What kind of snipe is that, we wondered? A moment's reflection, however, and we realised it was simply a folk-etymological version of the traditional character in these plays, the *Turkish Knight*, which during the course of time had come to be wrongly analysed as *Turki Shnight*, where **shnight* was understood as *snite*, a common variant form of *snipe*. Im Thurn records the hybrid formation *bunting-lark*[17] for the *corn bunting*; perhaps this is the countryman hedging his bets, the birds being proverbially similar (see Shakespeare's "I took this lark for a bunting" in *All's Well That Ends Well* II.v.6.).[18]

A CASE STUDY IN ORNITHOLOGICAL SEMANTICS

An analysis of the name *horse-matcher* enables us to demonstrate how a dialect name may be subject to etymological investigation.

The name is found in Richard Jefferies's *Wild life in a southern county* (1879): "Horse-matchers or stonechats also in summer often visit the rick-yard".[19] OED[20] lists the variants *horse-masher, horse-musher*,[21] *horse-match* and *horse-smatch*, and states that these forms denote the *stonechat* or *wheatear*.[22] *Smatch* is found in this sense uncompounded as early as 1544, and *stone-sma(t)ch/-smi(t)ch* from the later seventeenth century. There is also a German name, *stein-schmätzer*, independent testimony confirming the evidence of the early form *smatch*, that *smatch(er)* is the original form, the initial *s* having been lost in Jefferies's version, due to the immediately preceding *s* sound of *horse-*. As far as an etymology for the word goes, OED[23] will only say that "*smatch* is of obscure origin"; phonetically, however, there is no reason why *smatch* cannot be a variant of *smack*,[24] meaning *kiss (noisily)*, attested from the latter part of the seventeenth century; then there is a clear parallel with the element *-schmatzer*, and the German verb *schmätzen*, meaning *kiss noisily*. The first element seems to be *hoar* (meaning "grey or greyish-white"), which may be compared with the meaning "white rump" for *wheatear*. *Horse-match* would

29 *"Chats" from a 19th-century illustrated handbook: Whinchat (top), wheatear (below left) and stonechat (below right).*

then be an instance of false division from an original *hoar smatch*.[25]

THE ECOLOGICAL SIGNIFICANCE OF BIRD NAMES

An important application of the study of dialect names of birds is in the field of historical ecology which is concerned with species histories (changes in the status of organisms) and habitat changes. Such long-term biological patterns are usually only apparent from the interaction of different types of data. Generally, the data are concerned with land-use changes, as investigated through historical geography and agricultural history, and contemporary habitat preferences, environmental requirements and distribution patterns of species as revealed by the documentary record.[26] Information derived from an investigation of dialect names, although non-quantitative and only as good as the etymological analysis, may be used to *corroborate* other documentary sources, thus contributing to a fuller historical reconstruction, as has been demonstrated in the discussion of the place-name *Stintsford* (see Chapter 5).[27]

Two species which are sensitive to agricultural change, and thus can be regarded as 'indicators' of the biological consequences of the intensification of farming in recent decades, are the *stone curlew* and the *corncrake*. Five Wiltshire names for *stone curlew* have been recorded: *thick-kneed bustard*, which we discussed earlier, *great plover* an obvious colloquialism, *Norfolk plover*, a place-name association, and *pitchpenny* and *pitch-plug*. For *corncrake* we have *corndrake* and *drail*. (*Corndrake* is a good example of folk-etymology; *-crake* being no longer understood, it refers to the sound of the bird's call, the second syllable was changed to *drake*, which has obvious bird significance. *Drail* is simply a shortened version of the alternative name, *landrail*.) Both the *corncrake* and the *stone curlew* have declined as a result of agricultural change, the former through lack of traditional management of hay meadows and the latter from the intensive cultivation of downland. Evidence for the decline comes from localised documentary sources;[28] the dialect names for the species, with their wide distribution in Wiltshire, add a further geographical dimension to the decline as they testify to a time when the birds were widely known in the county.

Other ecologically significant species recorded in Wiltshire include *trammel hawk* for *peregrine falcon*; *barleybird, cuckoo's fool, cuckoo's mate, pea-jacket, snake-bird, valiant sparrow* and *hobby* for the *wryneck; redtail* for the

126

30 *Red-backed shrike, from Thomas Bewick's* A history of British birds, *1885 edition. Like the wryneck now greatly reduced in number but formerly a regular summer visitor to Wiltshire where it was known as* high mountain sparrow *or* horse-matcher.

redstart; and *high mountain sparrow* for the *red-backed shrike*. Of these, *trammel hawk* is probably one of the oldest, dating from a time when birds of prey were plentiful enough in Wiltshire to be taken for hawking.[29] The *trammel* was a type of fowler's net used especially for catching larks from the sixteenth century onwards; the more sporting way, however, was to take them with hawks as this revealing seventeenth century citation from OED[30] makes clear: "A Partridge taken in Flight, or a Lark dared with a Hawk, is worth ten taken with Nets, Springs and Trammels." The name is not likely to mean "species of hawk caught by means of trammel nets", so is probably a figurative usage, like Shakespeare's in which the falcon is seen as "trammelling up" the larks and other small birds (*Macbeth*, I.vii.3).

The seven names for the *wryneck*, which arrives in this country about the same time as the cuckoo, have possible significance when considering the history of this species, which is now virtually extinct in Wiltshire. Like the *redstart* (the dialect *redtail* explains the no longer comprehensible second element of the standard name, i.e. OE *steort, tail*) and the *red-backed shrike*, the *wryneck* is a summer visitor and Britain represents the extreme western limit of the range of all three, a range that has contracted in recent decades. The dialect names tell us nothing about the former abundance of the

127

species, but, as in the case of the *corncrake* and *stone curlew*, they provide an index of distribution so that we can say with some confidence that in the early nineteenth century at least, the bird was known throughout the county.[31]

31 *Wryneck, from Thomas Bewick's* A history of British birds, *1885 edition. This member of the woodpecker family, now virtually extinct in Britain, was formerly a regular summer visitor to Wiltshire, where it was known by at least seven different dialect names and local colloquialisms.*

WILTSHIRE NAMES FOR BIRDS

As with Chapter 6, on plant names, it seems appropriate to end this section with a full list of Wiltshire bird names. As we are dealing with fewer species than in the case of the plants, it has been possible to present a full list of the Wiltshire variants, not restricted to dialect names only, but including all local colloquialisms that we were able to locate from documentary sources. In this respect, the list which is given in Appendix 2 may be compared with the similar list recently published for the neighbouring county of Dorset.[32] Again, readers may like to try their hands at the etymology of some of the names for which we were unable to allocate space in the text.

NOTES

1 Since we wrote this chapter, Professor W. B. Lockwood's authoritative *Oxford book of British bird names* (1984) has appeared. This is the first comprehensive discussion of the names of British birds by a professional philologist and, as such, is of great importance. We are grateful to Professor Lockwood for reading our ornithological material and for suggesting several improvements. Occasionally, as in the *Stintsford* discussion (see Chapter 5) we have preferred to retain our alternative interpretation.

   The Oxford book of British bird names includes several dialect names of Wiltshire provenance, for example, *bank martin* (for *sand martin*) which Professor Lockwood notes "survives today in Wilts", and the form *Linnard* (for *linnet*) showing the final d/t alternation we have noted elsewhere. But undoubtedly the most interesting new [?] name from our point of view is *oar cock* listed as the Wiltshire variant of *war cock* a dialect name for the *water rail*. Professor Lockwood notes that the form *war cock* "to all appearances regularly continues the Middle English *c.*1420 *werkock*" cited by OED. (In fact, the name is attested earlier as part of the present day Lancashire place name *Warcockhill* as early as *c.*1280 – cited in EPNE under *wer-cock*.) Professor Lockwood is mistaken, however, when he continues "in the light of this, the Wilts. variant *oar cock* is evidently corrupt" for, as we have seen, this loss of initial *w* – is a diagnostic feature of the SW dialects and is to be expected in our county (see Chapter 2).

   The names, lore and literature of British birds have been well documented, the most recent popular account being Francesca Greenoak's *All the birds of the air* (1979). The standard works on local names for birds are Kirke Swann's *A dictionary of English and folk-names of British birds*, 1913 and Christine Jackson's *British names of birds*, 1968. Neither mentions a specific Wiltshire source. The principal Wiltshire sources drawn upon by Dartnell & Goddard are Aubrey's *Natural history of Wiltshire* (1656–1691), Maton's *Natural history of a part of the county of Wilts* (1843), Im Thurn's *Birds of Marlborough* (1870) and Smith's *Birds of Wiltshire* (1887). With the exception of Smith, who occasionally discusses the origin of a vernacular name, most of the authors simply list local variants. However, the etymology of many of the names can be established and it is apparent that most of the early Wiltshire dialect names are derived from observable morphological features of the species or from elements of their song or behaviour (including nest ecology). Many of the local names given in ordinary English date from the nineteenth century, being place associations or everyday colloquialisms.

2 For a recent county ornithological study see Buxton, J. 1981. *The birds of Wiltshire.*

3 The second element, *-ingale*, is modelled on *nightingale*.

4 These onomatopeic names for the *chaffinch* thus have a more lasting historical base than the two alternative, and probably more recent, variants given by Im Thurn (*pie finch*, descriptive of the pied plumage marking) and Smith (*chivy*, a likely corruption of *chaffy*).

5 OED entries associate *chide* with two other species – "the querulous call of quails" and a seventeenth century citation referring to partridges.

6 Dillon, P. J. 1977. "E. H. Goddard's natural history notes, 1873–1887". *The Wiltshire natural history magazine* 72: 3–9. W. B. Yapp (pers. comm.) points out that the call is most accurately likened to the noise made by the rapid pulling out of an angler's reel.

7 See OED under *bum* sb.[1]4, a rare word, defined in consequence somewhat vaguely, as "some protuberant part of a woman's dress" perhaps equivalent to *bum-roll*, defined by Halliwell as a "stuffed cushion worn by women about the hips", but this is a fashion of *c*.1600, suggesting that this name for the bird or rather of its nest, is of comparable antiquity. OED records *barrel-bird* as a nineteenth-century name for this bird.

8 *Pedigree: essays on the etymology of words from nature.* 1973, 72.

9 W. B. Yapp (pers. comm.) doubts if the inhabitants of Wiltshire distinguished between this species and the *herring gull* or the winter *black-headed gull.*

10 Whitlock, R. (1975) *Whitlock's Wessex* gives *barley-bird* as a dialect name for the *wryneck*; OED cites a nineteenth-century source for the same identification on the Isle of Wight.

11 Dillon, P. J. 1977. *op. cit.* 9.

12 Peirson, L. G. 1959. *Wiltshire birds.*

13 Morres, A. P. 1879. "On the occurrence of some of the rarer species of birds in the neighbourhood of Salisbury". *WAM* 18: 289–318. There is some mystery, however, about the precise status of this supposed variety of goldfinch. It is certainly not a sub-species and, in the absence of preserved specimens for examination, there must be some doubt about the authenticity of significantly large specimens.

14 OED, under *cheverel* sb.[2], cites Pennant's *Zoology* (1766): "A variety of goldfinch . . . called by the London bird catchers a cheverel from the manner in which it concludes its jerk", but it is difficult to see how this explains the name, unless perhaps it refers to the butting of a kid (see OED *cheverel* sb.[1] meaning *kid*).

15 See Dillon, P. J. and Jones, E. L. 1982. "Gwatkin's Wiltshire bird notebook, 1878–1938", *WAM* 77, 154–156.

16 Despite this lively trade, no other local colloquialisms have survived in the documentary record. However, evidence that the market for captive birds and their skins extended well beyond the British Isles survives in two local names with exotic associations: *Hummingbird* for *goldcrest* and *English parrot* for *green woodpecker*. Dartnell & Goddard record the former in use in north-west Wiltshire and Devon (Kirke Swann lists the Redcar district of Yorkshire), while Smith points to the latter as originating in the Salisbury district (which is very likely as Kirke Swann does not list it). Both are undoubtedly nineteenth century colloquialisms.

17 Whitlock, R. 1975 *op. cit.* gives *buntlark*.

18 Cited in the *Oxford dictionary of English proverbs*. 3rd edition, 1970: 18.

19 Chapter 10 – "The Woodpile".

20 See under *horse* 27b.

21 This form was doubtless influenced by dialect *horse-musheroom*; compare with the dialect pronunciation *musheroon* discussed elsewhere.

22 The position is complicated by the fact that *stonechat* seems to have been used as the Northern name for the bird called *wheatear* in the South (Grose, 1787. *op. cit.*), and, moreover, it is plain from OED's definition of *horsematch(er)*, that the dictionary regards *stone-chat* and *wheatear* as alternative names for the same species. This is confirmed by OED's definition of *steinchek*, the same citation which is used to define *smatch* so confidently as only meaning *wheatear*. However, in its definition at *stonechat*, OED does remark "also improperly applied to several allied species, as the *whinchat* . . . and the *wheatear*." – [even by its own lexicographers?].

This situation illustrates the problems of nomenclature which have to be resolved when dealing with any literary reference to species before 1758, when the Linnean system of classification (based on a binomial (generic and specific) name) was adopted by international agreement as a starting point for scientific naming. Moreover, it was many years before the terminology was fully standardised and printed lists of dialect names from any period, by their very nature, are beset by problems of interpretation. With regard to the species in question here, they are all members of the thrush family, *Turdidae: wheatear (Oenanthe oenanthe)*, *stonechat (Saxicola torquata)* and *whinchat (Saxicola rubetra)*. The confusion is understandable; they are all very similar in appearance, particularly the females, and their habitat requirements overlap so that all three often turn up in the same place. Other members of the thrush family which are visually similar to the "chats" are the *redstart (Phoenicurus phoenicurus)* and *black redstart (Phoenicurus ochrurus)*; the careful observer would distinguish them

131

by their characteristic russet tails. OED records a further complication by citing Jefferies (in *Bevis*, 1882), for *horse-matcher* as a name for *red-backed shrike*, a usage which occurs in Gloucestershire in the form *horse-match* (*Zoologist* 6 (1848)).

23 See under *smatch* sb.[2].

24 In this case of *smack* v.[2] (as OED *smatch* sb.[1] is of *smack* v.[2], i.e. the verb meaning *taste*). Many other examples of the *k* sound (spelled -*k* or -*ck*; described technically as the voiceless velar stop) varying in final position with the *ch* sound (spelled -*ch* or -*tch*; technically, the voiceless palatal affricate) could be cited. This variance explains the obvious semantic relation between such pairs as *bake* and *batch; wake* and *watch; strake* and *stretch; hack* and *(nut)-hatch; thack* (dialect for) *thatch* (and compare *Thakeham* – pronounced "thackam" – in Sussex, with *Thatcham* in Berkshire); compare also the variant place-name elements, OE *lacu* v. *læcc*, meaning *stream*; the former, with *k* sound, is the origin of the Wiltshire names, *Lackham* and *Lake* (*N.B.* the modern word *lake* is NOT connected with OE *lacu*), the latter, with *ch* sound, of the name *Latchmore* found in our county and elsewhere.

25 Professor W. B. Lockwood (personal communication).

26 The types of documentary record which are of particular interest to the historical ecologist are described by Rackham, O. 1980. "Documentary evidence for the historical ecologist", *Landscape history* 1: 29–33, and Sheail, J. 1980. *Historical ecology, the documentary evidence*. However, with very mobile animals such as birds, species histories need to be reconstructed with some care, particularly when it comes to "the great temptation to extrapolate the presumed mix and density of birds from modern information about habitat preferences and historical information about changes in habitat" (see Jones, E. L. 1981. "Reconstructing former bird communities", *Forth naturalist and historian* 6: 101–106).

27 The place of oral testimony in historical reconstruction, and objective criteria for evaluating its validity and limitations, are discussed fully in Thompson, P. 1978. *The voice of the past*.

28 See, for example, the discussions in Jones, E. L. 1966. "The Lambourn Downs" in Radford, M. C. *The birds of Berkshire and Oxfordshire*, and Dillon, P. J. and Jones, E. L. 1982. *op. cit.*

29 W. B. Yapp (pers. comm.) questions the association of *trammel hawk* with *peregrine. Peregrines*, he points out, would never have been plentiful in Wiltshire and they were not flown at partridges or larks. He thinks the dialect name may relate to the *hobby* or the *merlin*, two smaller birds of prey.

30 See under *trammel* sb.[1] 1b.

31 By the late nineteenth century the bird was in decline and Smith, *op.*

cit. 256–8, discusses the apparent paradox between the numerous provincial names for the species and its relative scarcity without perhaps appreciating the historical significance of the names.

32 Prendergast, E. D. V. 1982. "Dorset names for birds", *Proceedings of the Dorset Natural History and Archaeological Society*, 104: 33–37.

8

Specialised Lexicon: Dialect in Folklore

SEASONAL FESTIVALS

The Church calendar provided in former times many oppor-
tunities for popular enjoyment and the practice of folk-
customs which, with one or two exceptions (principally
Easter and Christmas customs, though mummers' plays
seem to be currently enjoying something of a revival) have
now disappeared, or else linger on in an extremely attenua-
ted form, for example, Shrove Tuesday, more popularly
known as Pancake Tuesday.

We consider first, two such now defunct festivals for which
there is nineteenth-century evidence and whose names are
quite properly of interest to dialect study.

On Shrove Tuesday small bands of shrovers would visit
various houses in the parish to ask for pancakes or the where-
withal to make them, or similar small gifts of food: eggs,
cheese, etc. Originally the prerogative of the genuinely
poor, "shroving was also a custom of young people and children, and in their hands it was not so much a way of asking
for charity as part of the traditional licence of merry-making
of the season".[1] Here are two shroving rhymes sung as soon
as the door has been opened:

> 1) We are come a-shroving
>   For a piece of pancake
>   For a piece of pancake
>   For a piece of chuckle[2] cheese,
>   Of your own making.

Is the pan hot?
Is the pan cold?
Is the peas in the pot
Nine days old?
Is the knives and forks whet?
Is the bread and cheese cut?
Is the best barrel tapped?
For we are come a-shroving.

(Berwick St. James a.1922)[3]

2) Knock, knock, knock,
Is the pan hot?
Is the pan cold?
Is the bread and cheese cut?
Is the best barrel tapped?
Please, Mam, I've come shroving!
Eggs and butter and lard so dear,
That's what makes I come a-shroving here.

(Shrewton 1899)[4]

Christina Hole[5] notes that "Polite requests for gifts were sometimes reinforced by more direct methods of persuasion, especially in the West of England, where the Shrovers often went out armed with stones or pieces of broken crockery, and used them as weapons to enforce generosity or punish refusals... In some Dorset villages, until about 1890, little gangs of children sang:

Here I come, I never came before,
If you don't give me a pancake,
I'll break down your door.

and then, without further delay, they joyfully hurled broken bits of crockery against the door."

136

Hence at Baverstock the day was known as *Lint Locke Day*: *Lint Locke* is a corruption, or more technically, an assimilated form of *Lent Crock*, as the following account by C. V. Goddard, former Rector of Baverstock, makes clear:

... this day used to be celebrated by the youths taking gates off their hinges and throwing them across the road, by throwing crocks and potsherds at the cottage doors, and by tying the leather thong by which the latch of the door was lifted to a stout piece of stick placed across the hole so that the inmates could not get out of the door in the morning.[6]

(All these pranks are common features of such "mischief nights", the last-mentioned was known in North Devon as "Dappy-Dooring".)[7] Manley in his *Folklore of Warminster* (1924) notes that the evening was called *Pansherd* or *Lent Crock* night, and his account of the proceedings is well worth quoting:

On Shrof Tuesday, the lads of the [Warminster] Common used to meet the Crockerton mill girls and "Thread the needle" all along the road, the front couple continually making an arch for the other couples to pass under. The words "Thread the needle" repeated thrice ended with "Noe, aye, noe", as a test of prospective marriage.

They also sang a song about "Poor Jack" and his mother's pancakes similar to this one recorded from Shrewton by C. V. Goddard in 1889:

> When Jack went to plough
> His mother made pancakes,
> She didn't know how,
> She tissed 'em, she tossed 'em,
> She made 'em so black,
> She put so much pepper [in]
> She poisoned poor Jack.
>
> (Shrewton 1889)[8]

137

32 *Clipping the church. A drawing of Rode church (Somerset) by W. W. Wheatley, 1848.*

Shrove Tuesday, Shrove Tuesday,
When Jack went to plow
His mother made pancakes,
She scarcely knew how,
She tossed them, she turned them,
She made them so black
With soot from the chimney
That poisoned poor Jack.

(Bradford-on-Avon version n.d.)[9]

Finally, in connexion with Shrove Tuesday customs, we must record that of "clipping the church", the goal of the 200-strong, "needle-threading", dancing procession at Warminster (as also at Hill Deverill and Bradford-on-Avon).[10] *Clip* is a now obsolete word for *embrace, hug* and, hence, *encircle*, and the custom consisted of the parishioners joining hands and "embracing" their church by moving round it in a large ring.

Writing in 1900, a Miss L. H. Johnson,[11] daughter of the former Vicar of Tilshead describes a custom which prevailed there until *c*.1850, called *Hocktide* (a festival which is still celebrated in neighbouring Berkshire at Hungerford):

On the second Tuesday after Easter the women and girls used to run after the men and tie their ankles together, also their wrists, leaving them helpless. They used to band themselves together for mutual protection or climb trees out of the way. Often they would sleep in the plantations and not return from their work in the fields. Next day the women were the victims. In the old days no-one was safe from this outrage. An old man who was asked the origin of this custom gave the following explanation: 'Ever so long ago a lot o' urd [i.e. *red*][12] folk from over the sea used to keep on a-comin'[13] and a-upsettin' o' we, so at last we 'ouldn' [i.e. *wouldn't*][14] stand it no longer, we up and at 'em, tied 'em up to postiz [i.e. two syllables][15] and cut their draughts [i.e. *throats*].'[16] By the red-haired folk from over the sea we are intended to understand the Danes i.e. Vikings; in Wiltshire folklore red hair was synonymous with Danish ancestry.[17]

This aetiological explanation is firmly rejected by Christina Hole[18] as a

later legend invented to account for the existence of a custom of which the true origin and meaning had been forgotten. It is probable that the ransom money collected during the Hocktide sports once went to provide a feast for the captors; but in the course of time, it came to be used for parish expenses, and was often a very useful contribution to the church funds.

The origin of the first element in the word *Hocktide* has been much disputed – OED says "Few words have received so much etymological and historical investigation. But the origin has not yet been ascertained..." It is tempting to connect one of the other *hock* words, i.e. *joint of the hind leg* (for example, of a horse), which derives ultimately, though somewhat irregularly, from OE *hōh, heel*,[19] especially in the context of a custom, the salient feature of which from the earliest days, was the binding together of ankles to prevent escape (as confirmed by the passage just quoted); it is not certain, however, that the earliest spellings of *Hock-day* will support such a relation with OE *hōh*.[20] The name of the festival is, incidentally, preserved in the surname, *Hocka-day*.

CUSTOMS EXPRESSING COMMUNAL DISAPPROVAL

An extraordinary practice expressing popular disapproval at marital irregularities of one kind or another, and one which seems to have died out only as recently as the turn of the century (see below), was known in the South West and Berkshire by two names exclusive to the region, the *skimmington (ride)* and the *hooset (hunt)*.[21]

Both names really refer to the same practice, or rather, series of practices (despite the efforts of some modern commentators to draw a distinction between the two). The "charivari" is an example of rough justice known to folk-custom throughout Britain and Europe; in its essentials it consisted of a procession of villagers parading an effigy of the couple, man or woman who had offended village morality in some way (for example by adultery, by wife-beating, or by allowing the wife to "wear the trousers", in those households where "the grey mare is the better horse"),[22] or of actors crudely representing the parties concerned, usually mounted astride a wooden pole (or on horseback, facing the tail),[23] accompanied by ear-splitting "rough music", i.e. the din of beaten pots, pans, and other similar domestic "instruments". At the climax of the procession, often outside the offending dwelling, the effigies were burned, shot or publicly defiled in some other way.

We are fortunate that in Wiltshire we have very early documentary evidence for this practice: from Calne in 1611,[24] nearby Quemerford in 1618,[25] and Marden in 1626[26] – these were all cases of public reproval of individuals; but the skimmington was also used as a vehicle for the reproval

33 *Plaster panel of c1590–1600 at Montacute House, Somerset, depicting the skimmington-ride.*

141

of groups or institutions and for the expression of community grievances, as in the contemporary popular protests of "The Western Rising" (1626–1632) against disafforestation and enclosure, the leaders of the rioters adopting the pseudonym of "Lady Skimmington", for example, at Braydon and Chippenham in 1631.[27] In neighbouring Somerset, at Montacute House, near Yeovil, there is even a very detailed plaster panel depicting a skimmington ride of this period, which is dated *c.*1590–1600.[28]

OED suggests that the word *skimmington* derives from *skimming* (-ladle) plus "*-ton,* as in *simpleton*, with the object of simulating a personal name", and cites an engraved frontispiece of 1639 depicting a woman beating her husband with a skimming-ladle, entitled "Skimmington and her husband", and the actors personating the object of the skimmington are frequently depicted as so equipped and belabouring their "husbands".[29]

Hooset, on the other hand (and the probably related Dorset (and Somerset) word, *ooser*, a grotesque animal-mask),[30] has no such apparent etymology, and there is uncertainty even over the initial spelling of the word, the forms *ooset* and *wooset* being also recorded; and what vowel sound is meant to be represented by *oo*? – as in StE *woo*, or as in StE *wood*? (Wiltshire sources also spell this vowel sound *ou*, and *u* as in "but".) According to EDD, at least, the *hooset*, as well as being the name for the procession or "hunt", is also the proper term for one of the chief, if not *the* chief, properties of the procession, "a horse's head curiously dressed up and carried about by men and boys." Nineteenth century Wiltshire records of a *hooset*[31] agree in repeating this important detail: the main exhibit of two *hoosets* witnessed by Carrington at Burbage in 1835 and Ogbourne St. George *c.*1840, was a seven-foot cross carrying a chemise on its arms and on its head a horse's skull with a pair of deer horns attached. Another "oosit hunt" witnessed at Ramsbury in 1868/1869 consisted of a procession "led by a man holding the skeleton of a horse's head on a stick, its jaws

34 *A typical "ooser" mask based on material from a local theatre production.*

143

made to open and shut by pulling a string."[32] Perhaps most significantly of all, when in 1943, E. R. Pole questioned a man who had taken part in a *hooset* in 1895 on the subject, his immediate response was "Do you want a horse's head? You know – a skeleton? I know where there is one which I can get you."[33] Ample parallels to this parading of a horse's skull can be cited, most notably the *Hodening Horse* and the Welsh *Mari Lwyd*.[34]

Our knowledge of Wiltshire dialect phonology can help establish the initial consonant of the word: the only initial sound that could lead to the variants *h, w* and – (zero), is an original *h*. (Compare StE *home*, found with dropped *h* in the form *ome* in Wiltshire dialect, and also with the secondary development of an added *w* in the form *wome*, by analogy with words such as StE *oak* and *old*, which can appear in our dialect as *woak* and *wold*.) So we can now conclude that *hooset* must be the correct form, and it seems to us that this is best explained, given the above evidence, as an eroded form of *horsehead*. The second *h* would quite regularly disappear at the beginning of an unstressed second syllable giving as starting-point, a form such as **hossed*; next, the final *d* sound would be unvoiced to *t* (a common enough occurrence in this unstressed position)[35] to give **hosset* or similar, and then there remains only the uncertain quality of the vowel to be accounted for.[36]

KIT CANDLESTICK

The eerie though natural phenomenon known commonly as *Will-o'-the-wisp* or *Jack-o'-lantern*, is recorded by Aubrey in his *Natural history of Wiltshire* (1656–91) as "called by the vulgar '*Kit of the Candlestick*'",[37] an expression recorded by C. V. Goddard in the form "*Tick Candlestick*".[38] The first word is a pet-form of the name *Christopher*, which makes an exact parallel with the *Will* and *Jack* of the other two expressions (*wisp* here, incidentally, means "*a bunch or twisted bundle of hay or straw for burning as a torch*").[39]

144

35 *An early 20th-century postcard from a painting by George Pritchard depicting the moonrakers folktale.*

FOLK-TALES

The folk-tale of the "Moonrakers", that has given us the jocular name for Wiltshiremen, is recorded as early as 1787 by Grose in his *Provincial glossary with a collection of local proverbs and popular superstitions*: "Some Wiltshire rustics, as the story goes, seeing the figure of the moon in a pond, attempted to rake it out", but as OED drily comments, "In Wiltshire a more complimentary turn is given to the story: the men were caught raking a pond for kegs of smuggled brandy, and put off the revenue men by pretending folly."[40] Just four years later in a letter to *The Western counties magazine*, a farmer from Poulshot claimed that the pond in question was to be found in his village,[41] but it is fruitless to speculate on its precise whereabouts, for this story has all the hall-marks of a traditional folk-tale of the "Wise Men of Gotham" type, and indeed. H. C. Brentnall noted an interesting and presumably independent, French version printed in the 1930s featuring the *Pescalunes*, and commented that "the existence of this parallel makes it impossible to accept the consoling accretion to our local story, which turns the ingenuous yokel into a nimble-witted smuggler".[42] We should, rather, compare the still current sense of *moonshine*, earlier, *moonshine in the water* (found for example in Shakespeare's *Love's Labours Lost* V.ii.208), i.e. "an appearance without substance; something unsubstantial or unreal" (OED). Nor must we forget the very relevant sense, 'smuggled spirits', also first recorded by Grose in 1785.[43]

"The Wise Men of Gotham" tales are the classic English representatives of the international "Noodle Villagers" tale-type found early in Arabian tales, and making an early appearance in Western literature via Petrus Alphonsus's early twelfth century Latin collection of Eastern tales entitled, somewhat misleadingly, *Disciplina clericalis*; an Anglo–French translation of this work existed by the end of the century.[44] Another "Wise Men of Gotham" tale, the "Cuckoo-Penners", which relates how, in an effort to cage in

36 *Contemporary pub sign from Pewsey depicting the moonrakers folktale.*

the cuckoo (and thus, incidentally, indefinitely prolong the spring), the village noodles simply penned it in with a high fence round the bush on which it had alighted, can be found in our, as in many other counties.[45] J. E. Field in his highly speculative *The Myth of the pent cuckoo* (1913), quotes an unnamed "village poet of recent times" who identifies a horse-shoe-shaped earthwork near Downton as the original "Cuckoo-Pen", but the authenticity of this identification is very suspect, for the poem simply attributes all the traditional follies of the Gothamites to "The Wise Men of Downton". John Field (*not* the same author!) in his *English field names: a dictionary* (1972), lists 13 *Cuckoo Pen* names, of which Gloucestershire boasts 7 and Oxfordshire 4: none are given for Wiltshire. PNW, however, lists a *Cuckoo Pen* in its collection of minor and field-name elements, but, unfortunately, does not locate it – perhaps it is to be identified with that listed under Ashton Keynes in the WANHS Library's three-volume interleaved PNW compiled by the late T. R. Thomson. *Cuckoo Bush* is another field-name which, in the Nottinghamshire Gotham, at least, alludes to the same story; there was once a field so named (no longer extant?) near Notton, Lacock, according to the unpublished manuscript gazetteer of Wiltshire place-names compiled *c*.1860 by J. E. Jackson, also in the WANHS Library.

In our county, the Noodle Village par excellence is Bishops Cannings and several of these tales may be found in reconstructed nineteenth century dialect form in our Appendix 3 below, and the extensive Commentary thereto.

A final folk-tale purports to explain the alleged local Aldbourne name of *sea woodcock* for the *dabchick*, a bird of peculiar interest to the natives of that village who were and are themselves called Aldbourne dabchicks; after listing several popular names for the bird, Im Thurn concludes:

The last in the rather long list of country names is rather a peculiar one. Connected with it is the following anecdote, which I have from a gamekeeper, a native of Aldbourne, and a firm believer in the fact that "sea woodcock" is the scientific name of this bird. A little grebe appeared in a farmyard pond at Aldbourne. No-one knew what this, as they supposed, "rara avis" was; a bedridden old man, who was supposed to be possessed of a good deal of ornithological knowledge, was accordingly wheeled out in his armchair to give his opinion. A good deal of hesitation ensued, and the "man of science" at last pronounced it a "sea woodcock", and by this name it has since been known.[46]

PROVERBS

Proverbs are an important category of folk speech and, in addition to those already cited in passing, we conclude this section with a few of specifically Wiltshire provenance.[47] In his DHS Eric Partridge (under *horse-ladder*) gives: *"to send for a horse-ladder"* i.e. *to send on a fool's errand.* He labels it a rural colloquialism, especially a Wiltshire one, records its currency as mid eighteenth to early nineteenth century, and continues with this additional information: "The victim was told that it was needed 'to get up the horses' (or in Grose's 1796 version: 'to finish a hay-mow' i.e. hay-stack)". There is a similar proverb recorded by Ray in 1678, but given a regrettably sexist application: "When an ass climbs a ladder, we may find wisdom in women".

37 *A Gotham cuckoo-penner depicted in a woodcut on the title page of* The merry tales of the mad-men of Gotam (*by Andrew Boorde*), *1630.*

Augustus Hare's *Memorials of a quiet life* (1872), the biography of a country clergyman who spent his last years at Alton Barnes, records the following unflattering opinion offered by the village carpenter as one of the reasons for the local manifestations of the machine-breaking riots of 1830: "They are so ignorant in this county, there's many who boast that they do not know a great 'A' from a turnip." This is a Wiltshire variant of a proverb first recorded in 1401 in the form "I knew not an 'A' from the wyndmylne (i.e. a sign in the shape of a windmill used like the modern asterisk), ne a 'B' from a bole foot". In 1980, we heard an Avebury variant of this form from Mrs G Rawlins in the form "not to know 'A' from a bull's foot".

Recently a friend informed us that her father a Wiltshireman, used to use the expression *"as dry as a kex"*, and this proverbial phrase is, in fact, first recorded by the *Oxford dictionary of English proverbs* as early as 1553 in the work of the Hampshireman, Nicholas Udall. In a play, quite possibly by the same man, entitled *Respublica* (1553), the character, People, who naturally speaks in a South-Western dialect, says: "An ye bydde mee, chill squease hym as drie as a kyxe". A *kex* is a widespread dialect word for the dry hollow stem of several umbelliferous plants, for example, *cow parsley, hemlock* etc., but the proverb is perhaps essentially South Western in its distribution, being found, for instance in chapter 17 of Hardy's *Tess of the D'Urbervilles* (1891), and Jefferies, in his *Round about a great estate* (1880), refers to "Cutting a dry *gicks* so that it should be open at either end, like a tube."[48]

NOTES

1 Hole, C. 1979. *A dictionary of British folk customs*. Since this chapter was written Professor John Widdowson has delivered the sixth Katherine Briggs Memorial Lecture to the Folklore Society (in November 1986), entitled "English dialects and folklore: a neglected heritage," published in *Folklore* 98:1 (1987): 41–52.

2 *Chuckle*, an assimilated form of *truckle*, under the influence of the following *cheese*. A *truckle cheese* is a small, barrel-shaped cheese.

3 *WAM* 50 (1942): 39, where it is said to be taken from Udal, J. S. 1922. *Dorsetshire folk lore*, from a manuscript given to Udal by the Rev. W. K. Kendall of East Lulworth.

4 *WAM* 50 (1942): 40; source C. V. Goddard.

5 Hole, C. 1979 *op. cit.*

6 *WAM* 50 (1942): 40

7 Hole, C. 1979 *op. cit.*; see further Opie, I and P. 1959 *The lore and language of schoolchildren*.

8 *WAM* 50 (1942): 39

9 *WAM* 50 (1942): 26; source *Wiltshire cuttings* 16: 36 (WANHS Library).

10 For Hill Deverill, see Manley, V. S. 1924. *Folk lore of the Warminster district*; for Bradford-on-Avon, see *WAM* 50 (1942): 26

11 *WAM* 50 (1942): 29

12 For similar metathesis see Chapter 2, "Other changes . . ."

13 For the present participle in *a-*, see Chapter 3, "Participles".

14 For loss of initial *w-*, see Chapter 2, "Semi-vowels".

15 For the extra-syllable plural of nouns ending in *-st*, see Chapter 3, "Plurals".

16 For the initial consonant change, see Chapter 2, "Initial consonants".

17 *WAM* 50 (1942): 29, "Crossed with the Danes"; see also D&G under *Dane*.

18 Hole, C. 1979 *op. cit.*: 145

19 i.e. OED *hock* sb^2. See further Chambers, E. K., 1903. *The medieval stage*: 154–6

20 See OED under *hock-day: hoce-* (*c.*1175); *hoke-* (1219); *hocke-* (*a.*1252, from a Glastonbury document); *hokke-* (*c.*1330). For further remarks on the development of the phonology of OE *hōh*, see OED's note under *hough*. The derivation is discussed by Axton, R. 1974. *European drama of the middle ages*: 42: "Hox Tuesday seems to connect it with some ox festival . . . The Coventry Annals date the invention of Hox Tuesday 1416–7. It seems that at that time the historical episode [i.e. St Bride's Night, 1002] (surviving perhaps in ballad form) was recast in terms of a folk custom known as 'hoxing' or 'hocking'. This was concerned with a battle of the sexes and seems to have lost any connection it ever had with an ox (except perhaps in the ceremony of *binding* a man . . .)." For the form *hough* note Thomas Heywood's "A woman killed with kindness" (1603): "Does not that rascal Wendoll go on legs / That thou must cut off? Hath he not hamstrings / That thou must *hough*?" (II.iii.171ff.)

21 There are studies of this folk-custom by Thompson, E.P. 1972.

"'Rough music': le charivari Anglais", *Annales* 27.2:285–312; Ingram, M. J. 1984. "Ridings, rough music and 'the reform of popular culture' in early modern England", *Past and present* 105: 79–113; and Underdown, D. E. 1985. "The taming of the scold", in *Order and disorder in early modern England* (edited by Fletcher, A. and Stevenson, J.): especially pp. 130–3. The best-known literary instances are in Samuel Butler's *Hudibras* (1663), II.ii; Thomas Hardy's *The mayor of Casterbridge* (1902), chapter 39; Flora Thompson's *Lark rise to Candleford* (1945), chapter 8. There is also a description of a charivari against a violent wife in Andrew Marvell's "Last instructions to a painter", lines 387–9 (Margoliouth, H. M. (ed.) 1971. *Poems and letters of Andrew Marvell* (3rd edition): I.156–7. See also Seal, G. 1987, "A 'hussitting' in Berkshire," *Folklore* 98 (1): 91–4.

22 See Wilson, F. P. 1970. *The Oxford dictionary of English proverbs* (3rd edition), under "Grey mare is the better horse, The", and note 34 below.

23 For a discussion of this particular motif, see Mellinkoff, R. 1973. "Riding backwards: theme of humiliation and symbol of evil", *Viator* 4: 153–76.

24 See Alford, V. *Folklore* 70 (1959): 505

25 Cunnington, B. H. *Folklore* 41 (1930): 287–90; reprinted in Cunnington, B. H. 1932. *Records of the county of Wiltshire*.

26 Cunnington, B. H. 1932 *op. cit.*, note 16.

27 See Sharp, B. 1980. *In contempt of all authority*, chapter 4, which supersedes all previous accounts.

28 See Pevsner, N. 1958. *South and west Somerset* (Buildings of England), and *Victoria history of Somerset* (1974): vol. 3. A painting of a similar scene by the mid-seventeenth century Dutch artist Jean Molenaer is illustrated in Röhrich, L. 1973. *Lexikon der sprichwörtlichen Redensarten*. sv. Pantoffelheld.

29 Compare also, from the mid-sixteenth century play, *Ralph Roister Doister* (IV.iv.19–20), set in the West Country: "And I with our skimmer will fling him one flap", and the earlier (*a*.1450): "proud Pernelle ... wolde ... with hir skumour reeche him on the heued", from Lydgate's *Mumming at Hertford*.

30 Cawte, E. C. 1978. *Ritual animal disguise*, is essential reading on animal-headed figures, including the hobby-horse (and Salisbury's famous "Hob-nob"). Mr Cawte deals with the *ooser* briefly on p. 153, referring to *Notes and queries for Somerset and Dorset*, vols. 2 and 3 (1891–2), and citing the following amusing anecdote from Child, F. 1844. *The spinster at home in the close of Salisbury*: 393–5, as proof that *ooser* "was certainly pronounced *wurser* in Hampshire": "Saw ye ever a Worser?" cried a showman at Weyhill Fair. Those who paid a half-

penny were shown, not an ooser, but a starved pig. Though cheated, they had to admit that they had never seen a *worser* pig (Cawte, E. C. 1978. *op. cit.* 252–3).

31 These three reports are collected in Carrington, F. A. 1854. "On certain Wiltshire customs', *WAM* 1: 88–9

32 The resemblance to the Morris and hobby horses will not have escaped the reader.

33 *WAM* 51 (1943)

34 See Owen, T. 1974. *Welsh folk customs*; Hole, C. 1979. *op. cit.*, under *Hodening*; Alford, V. 1959. *op. cit.* The most plausible translation of the Welsh *Mari Lwyd* is *Grey mare* – this would bring the Welsh custom very much into line with the *hooset* hunt. *Grey mare* is the term of opprobrium directed against the woman in those ménages where "the grey mare is the better horse" (see Wilson, F. P. 1970. *loc. cit.*).

35 Ross, A. S. C. 1965. *Etymology*: 136, notes that "Unvoicing of final consonants is found sporadically in most areas [in Middle English times], but is very common in the West Midlands (especially *t* for *d*), for example, *hundret*." SED records *secont* for *second* from four of the Wiltshire localities. Compare the state of flux attested by the alternative StE spellings: *burned, burnt, smelled, smelt*; etc.

36 In a personal communication, Dr Wakelin has noted a precise parallel in the spelling *Dooset* for *Dorset*, in a document dated 1802.

37 Britton's edition, 1847 (reprinted 1969): 16. OED attests the name from the late-seventeenth century.

38 *WAM* 50 (1942): 29.

39 See OED under *wisp* sb[1]. 3a.

40 For this flattering interpretation see Smith, A. C. 1874. 'On Wiltshire traditions, charms and superstitions', *WAM* 14: 326–7.

41 Cited in Gandy, I. 1960. *Round about the little steeple*: 21.

42 Brentnall, H. C. 1939. 'French moonrakers', *WAM* 48: 466–7. A related motif is attested much earlier in the late-twelfth century fable of "The fox and the reflection of the moon" by Marie de France. The fox thinks the moon's reflection in the pond is an enormous cheese and attempts to get at it by drinking the pond dry, but he drinks so much he drops dead (Ewert, A. and Johnson, R. C. eds. 1942. *Marie de France Fables*, no. 31).

43 Cited in DHS under *moonshine*. See also now Pitcher, E. W. 1986. "Illicit spirit in OED", *Notes and queries* NS 33.1: 21.

44 For the "Wise men of Gotham" tales, see Clouston, W. A. 1888. *The book of noodles*, for other such stories located at Bishops Cannings, see Appendix 3, "The Cannings Vawk" and further, Thompson, S. 1955. *Motif-index of folk literature*. For Petrus Alphonsus, see Hermes, E. (trans. Quarrie, P. R.) 1977. *The Disciplina clericalis of*

Petrus Alfonsi. The tale of "The countryman and the little bird' is no. XXII, pp. 141–2 and pp. 186–7, n. 116.

45 The early currency of this particular motif is also incidentally attested in a nickname occurring in a Staffordshire assize roll of 1293 which refers to one Henry *Pendecrow/Pundecrow* from OE *pyndan, pen + crāwe, crow* (cited by Reaney, P. H. 1967. *The origin of English surnames*: 289). In recent years the spring fair at Downton has been revived as the Cuckoo Fair, a name by which it was apparently known before it was abandoned in 1919. The explanation for the name, that a cuckoo was captured and released at the fair, is recorded by the Downton Women's Institute, in their unpublished scrapbook history, *c*.1965.

46 For a somewhat different version of this tale, where the bird is correctly identified as a *dabchick*, and this pronouncement is said to be the origin of the sobriquet by which the villagers of Aldbourne are traditionally known, see Wiltshire, K. 1975. *Wiltshire folklore*: 132. See also Gandy, I. 1975. *The heart of a village*: 16–7. But note that Kirke Swann lists *sea-woodcock* as the Shetland name for the *godwits*. As for the "land woodcock", Greenoak gives *quis* as the Wiltshire name, though D&G under *quest, quist* state that this is the name of the woodpigeon, citing Smith: "The Wilts labourers invariably call it ... the *Quisty*". EPNE further points out that the place-name element OE *cocc, cock*, "probably often denotes a wild bird such as the woodcock"; where it certainly does so is in those names formed from the compound OE *cocc-rodu*, "a cock-road or (artificial) clearing in a wood where woodcock were netted"; it is a fairly common element in field- and minor names, and there are at least three in our county: *Cockroad Plantation* (near Atworth); *Cock Road* (near Horningsham); and *Cockroad Cottages* (near Rowde). (Compare OED under *rode* v[2].2 "of woodcock: to perform a regular evening flight during the breeding season", also under *roading* vbl. sb[2].)

47 Unless stated otherwise, proverbs are cited from Wilson, F. P. 1970. *op. cit.* See a recent study of proverbs by Smith, J. B. 1982. 'Cockaigne and Lubberland: on the survival of some popular themes and forms in English', *Quinquereme* 5.2: 226–40.

48 Chapter 7. Such forms with initial *g*- sound may give further weight to the suggestion that the word is of Celtic derivation (see ODEE), as this is a familiar Welsh initial mutation pattern (i.e. *c → g*). The form *kelk* is also recorded for Wiltshire by Grigson. OE *cammoc, commuc* is the old name for *restharrow* (Grigson gives this for Wiltshire; D&G, however, did not hear the word, merely citing its appearance in Davis's *General view of the agriculture of Wiltshire* (1809), though they *were* familiar with *cammocky*: "Tainted or ill-flavoured, as cheese or milk when the cows have been feeding on cammock") and also, according to

EPNE, for *kex* or *cow-parsley*, citing a Wiltshire field-name, *le Commek* (whose precise location we have not been able to trace from PNW).

Appendix 1

WILTSHIRE NAMES FOR PLANTS

The list is arranged in four columns giving: the scientific name (nomenclature standardised on Rose, F. 1981. *The wild flower key*); the common name; the Wiltshire variant(s); the regional occurrence of the variant where specified. The source for all items in the list is D&G.

Anagallis arvensis	Scarlet pimpernel	*Bird's eye*	SWi
		Numpinole	NWi
		Ploughman's weatherglass	Barford
		Shepherd's weatherglass	NWi; SWi
		Weatherglass	NWi; SWi
Ballota nigra	Black horehound	*Double-dumb-nettle*	Charlton
		Wurral, worral	Somerset border
		Paper beech	NWi
Briza media	Quaking grass	*Double-grass*	
		Quakers	NWi; SWi
		Shakers	NWi; SWi
		Wagtails	NWi; SWi
		Wagwants, wegwants	NWi; SWi
		Wing-wang	NWi; SWi
Caltha palustris	Marsh marigold	*Butter-flower*	
		Claut	NWi
		Crazy bets	NWi; SWi
		Drunkards	Somerset border
		Gilty cap	Zeals
Capsella bursa-pastoris	Shepherd's-purse	*Pickpocket*	NWi; SWi
Centaurea nigra	Black knapweed	*Dromedary*	Barford
		Hardhead	NWi; SWi
		Loggerums	

157

Chelidonium majus	Greater Celandine	*Wart-wort*	NWi; SWi
Chrysanthemum leucanthemum	Oxeye daisy	*Crazy bets*	Hamptworth
		Mathern, mauthern	NWi
		Maudlin	NWi
		Moon-daisy, moons	NWi; SWi
Euphorbia helioscopia	Sun spurge	*Saturday's pepper*	
		Saturday-nights-pepper	
Fumaria officinalis	Common fumitory	*Dicky-birds*	Deverill
		Fevertory	SWi
		Lady's shoe	Barford
Genista tinctoria	Dyer's greenweed	*Wood-wax*	NWi; SWi
Heracleum sphondylium	Hogweed	*Altrot, eltrot*	SWi
		Hill-trot	
		Clog-weed	NWi
Juglans regia	Walnut	*Bannut*	
Lamium album	White dead-nettle	*Deaf nettle*	SWi
		Dumb nettle	Charlton
		Dunch nettle	Barford
Lamium purpureum	Red dead-nettle	*Dunch nettle*	SWi
Lemna minor	Common duckweed	*Creed*	NWi
Lolium perenne	Perennial rye-grass	*Soldiers- sailors- tinkers- tailors*	
Mentha pulegium	Pennyroyal	*Organy*	
Nuphar lutea	Yellow water-lily	*Blobbs*	
		Water-blobbs	Mere
Onobrychis viciifolia	Sainfoin	*French grass*	Enford
Orchis mascula	Early-purple orchid	*Dandy-goslings*	NWi
		Grandigoslings	NWi
		Goslings	NWi
		Grampha-griddle-goosey-ganders	Zeals
		Underground-shepherd	Charlton
Papaver rhoeas	Poppy	*Blind-man*	
		Red-weed	NWi; SWi
		Soldiers	SWi
		Thunderflower	SWi
Plantago major	Greater plantain	*Wayside-bread*	
		Fightin-cocks	
Populus tremula	Aspen	*Aps*	NWi
Prunus spinosa	Blackthorn	*Hedge-peg*	Marlborough
		Hilp	NWi
		Pick	
		Slan	
		Snags	Salisbury
Ranunculus sp.	Buttercups in general	*Crazy bets*	SWi
		Crazy man	Clyffe Pypard
		Gilcup	SWi
		Gawl-cup	Malmesbury

158

Ranunculus arvensis	Corn buttercup	*Crowpeck*	Clyffe Pypard
		Hedge-hog	SWi
Ranunculus repens	Creeping buttercup	*Crazy-more*	Devizes; Huish
		Crazy-mar	Devizes; Huish
		Crazy-moir	Devizes; Huish
Rubus fruticosus	Bramble	*Blackberry-moucher*	Huish
		Moocheso	SWi
		Penny mouchers	NWi
Sambucus ebulus	Dwarf elder	*Dane's blood*	
Sedum telephium	Orpine	*Midsummer men*	NWi; Farley
Stellaria holostea	Greater stichwort	*Mother-Shimbles-*	
		snick-needles	Zeals
		Nightingale	Hampshire border
		Poppies	Lyneham
		Shirt-buttons	Deverill
		Snake-flower	Barford
		Snaps, snapjacks	SWi
		White flowers	Huish
Tragopogon pratensis	Goat's beard	*Jack-go-to-bed-at-noon*	NWi; SWi
Taxus baccata	Yew	*Snotter-gall*	NWi; SWi
Ulex europeaus	Gorse	*Fingers-and-thumbs*	SWi
Ulmus sp.	The elms	*The Wiltshire weed*	
Umbelliferae	The carrot family	*Kecks, keeks*	NWi; SWi
		Kecksey	NWi; SWi
		Gix, gicksies	NWi; SWi
Valeriana dioica	Marsh valerian	*Cat-finger-leaf*	Huish
		Gooseberry-pie	SWi
Valeriana officinalis	Common valerian	*Cherry-pie*	SWi
Viburnum lantana	Wayfaring-tree	*Coventree*	
		Whitty-tree	
Viburnum opulus	Guelder-rose	*Snowball tree*	
Vicia sp.	The vetches	*Blue thatch*	
		Red thatch	
		Yellow thatch	
		Lent thatch	NWi
		Thatches, thetches	NWi
Viola tricolor	Wild pansy	*Love-an'-idols*	NWi; SWi
		Loving idols	NWi; SWi
		Nuffin-idols	NWi; SWi
		Loveidolds	NWi; SWi

Appendix 2

WILTSHIRE NAMES FOR BIRDS

The list is arranged in four columns giving: the common name; the Wiltshire variant(s); the regional occurrence of the variant where specified, and the source of information. Wiltshire variants are listed chronologically and the source of the earliest citation is listed, abbreviated thus:

Aubrey, J.	1656–1691	*The natural history of Wiltshire*	Aub.
Lansdowne, MSS	1695	(listed in Dartnell and Goddard)	Lan MSS.
Britton, J.	1825	*The beauties of Wiltshire* (word list in Volume III)	JB.
Akerman, J. W.	1842	*Glossary of provincial words and phrases in use in Wiltshire.*	Aker.
Maton, G.	1843	*The natural history of a part of the county of Wiltshire.*	Mat.
Im Thurn, E.	1870	*The birds of Marlborough*	ImT.
Jefferies, R.	1879	*Wild life in a southern county*	RJ(i).
Jefferies, R.	1880	*Round about a great estate*	RJ(ii).
Jefferies, R.	1882	*Bevis*	RJ(iii).
Smith, A. C.	1887	*Birds of Wiltshire*	Smith
Slow, E.	1890	*Glossary of Wiltshire words*	ES.
Dartnell, G. E. and Goddard, E. H.	1892–1899	Contributions towards a Wiltshire Glossary. *WAM* 26: 84–171, 293–314; 27: 124–159, 30: 233–270	D&G.
Hony, G. B.	1914	Local names of birds in *MSS* catalogue of birds in the Museum. Devizes Museum	GBH.
Whitlock, R.	n.d.	*Whitlock's Wessex*	RW.
Greenoak, F.	1979	*All the birds of the air*	FG.

Dabchick	*Didapper*	SWi	Mat.
	Dipper		ImT.
	Sea woodcock		ImT.
	Diedapper	Salisbury	D&G
	Dapcheck		GBH.

Heron	*Hern*		ImT.
	Moll'ern	NWi	RJ (ii).
	Jack	NWi	Smith
	Molly heron	NWi	RJ (ii).
	Jack ern	NWi	Smith
Tufted duck	*Pie curr*		GBH.
Marsh harrier	*Dun pickle*		FG.
Hobby	*Rook hawk*		Smith
Peregrine falcon	*Trammel hawk*		Smith
Kestrel	*Stannel hawk*		ImT.
	Wind hover		ImT.
Corncrake	*Corndrake*	Warminster, NWi	D&G
	Drail	NWi	D&G.
Moorhen	*Water hen*		ImT.
	Marsh hen		ImT.
Woodcock	*Quis*		FG.
Common sandpiper	*Summer snipe*	NWi; SWWi	D&G.
Stone curlew	*Thick-kneed bustard*		Mat.
	Great plover		ImT.
	Pitch-penny & Pitch-plug		RW.
	Norfolk plover		ImT.
Common gull	*Barley sower*	SWi	Smith
Woodpigeon	*Quest*	NWi; SWi	D&G
	Quist	NWi; SWi	D&G
	Quisty	NWi; SWi	D&G
Barn owl	*Screech owl*		Mat.
	White owl		ImT.
	Church owl		ImT.
	Hissing owl		ImT.
Tawny owl	*Brown owl*		ImT.
Long eared owl	*Horned owl*		ImT.
	Long horned owl		ImT.
Nightjar	*Goatsucker*		ImT.
	Fern owl		ImT.
Swift	*Screech*		ImT.
	Screech devil		ImT.
	Screech martin		ImT.
	Screamer		ImT.
	Devil screecher	NWi; SWi	D&G.
	Screecher		GBH.
Green woodpecker	*Rainbird*		ImT.
	Popinjay		ImT.
	English parrot	Salisbury	Smith
	Yuckle	NWi; SWi	D&G.
	Yoppingal		GBH.
	Yaffingale		FG.
Great spotted woodpecker	*Black woodpecker*		Smith
	Grey woodpecker		Smith
Wryneck	*Barley bird*		RW.
	Cuckoo's mate		ImT.
	Peajacket		RW.
	Snake bird		ImT.

	Valiant sparrow		Smith
	Hobby	SWi	D&G.
	Cuckoo's fool	NWi	D&G.
Sand martin	*Quar martin*	NWi	RJ (i).
Hooded crow	*Royston crow*		Aub.
	Gray crow		Aub.
	Beckhampton grey crow		ImT.
Magpie	*Maggotty pie*		Lan MSS.
Jay	*Joy bird*	Savernake	D&G.
Blue tit	*Blue tomtit*		ImT.
Long-tailed tit	*Long-tailed titmouse*		ImT.
	Bottle tom		ImT.
	Bottle tit		ImT.
	Long-tailed pie		ImT.
	Bombarrel tit	NWi	RJ (ii).
	Huckmuck	NWi; SWi	Smith
Tree creeper	*Treemouse*	SWi	Smith
	Tree climber		GBH.
Wren	*Jenny-pooper*		RW.
	Jenny wren		ImT.
	Titty-wren	NWi	D&G.
	Nanny-fodger	NWi	D&G.
	Nunny-fudger	NWi	D&G.
	Cutty	SWi	D&G.
	Cutty-wren		RW.
	Scutty		GBH.
Mistle thrush	*Storm cock*		ImT.
	Shrike cock		ImT.
	Squeaking thrush	NWi	D&G.
	Ichila-pea	NWi	D&G.
	Rattle thrush	Salisbury	D&G.
	Russell thrush	Salisbury	D&G.
	Jay pie		FG.
Fieldfare	*Veldvare*		Aker.
	Veldever	Clyffe	D&G.
	Vulver	Huish	D&G.
	Velt	NWi	D&G.
	Vichver		GBH.
	Felt		GBH.
	Velverd		FG.
Song thrush	*Throstle*		ImT.
Wheatear	*Furze hawker*	NWi	Smith
	Horse snatcher	NWi	Smith
Stonechat	*Horse matcher*	NWi	RJ (i).
	Furze robin	NWi	Smith
Whinchat	*Furze chat*		ImT.
	Vuzz chat		GBH.
Redstart	*Redtail*		ImT.
Grasshopper warbler	*Mowing-machine bird*	Mere	Smith
Reed warbler	*Reed sparrow*		ImT.
Sedge warbler	*Brook sparrow*		RJ (ii).
	Johny chider	SWi	D&G
	Chan chider	SWi	D&G

163

	Jan chider	SWi	ES.
	Mocking bird		GBH.
Blackcap	*Small nightingale*		ImT.
Garden warbler	*Nettle creeper*		Smith
Whitethroat	*Nettle creeper*		ImT.
Lesser whitethroat	*Nettle creeper*		Smith
Willow warbler	*Yellow wren*		ImT.
	Willow wren		ImT.
Wood warbler	*Jacky-dinah*	SWi	D&G.
Goldcrest	*Humming-bird*	Huish	D&G.
Meadow pipit	*Cheeper*		ImT.
	Titlark		ImT.
Pied wagtail	*Dishwasher*		JB.
	Water wagtail		ImT.
	Scullery maids		GBH.
Goldfinch	*Chevil*		Smith
	Chevril		Smith
	Three-pound-tenner		Smith
Linnet	*Red linnet*		ImT.
	Brown linnet		ImT.
	Grey linnet		ImT.
	Greater redpoll		ImT.
Bullfinch	*Hoop*		JB.
	Red hoop	NWi	D&G.
Chaffinch	*Chink*	SWi	D&G.
	Chivy	SWi	Smith
	Pie finch		ImT.
Corn bunting	*Bunting lark*		ImT.
	Buntlark		RW.
Yellowhammer	*Yellow ammer*		ImT.
Reed bunting	*Reed sparrow*		GBH.
Red-backed shrike	*High-mountain sparrow*		RW.
	Horse-matcher		RJ (iii).

Appendix 3

SPECIMEN TEXTS

Introduction

The following Specimen Texts have been selected to illustrate the chronological development of dialect in Wiltshire, and in order to move away from the consideration of discrete items to a study of passages of *continuous* speech.

We have avoided any illustration from the Medieval period, partly as until recently there was no suitable published material which could be assigned a Wiltshire provenance (see remark in Chapter 1), and partly from the inordinate amount of commentary that any such passage of Middle English would require. We begin, therefore, in the Early Modern period, with a text which claims to reproduce specifically the dialect of Wiltshire (and does so more reliably than most stage attempts at South-Western dialect: see Commentary, and compare Chapter 1, section "Historical representations"), we continue with early and late nineteenth-century texts, and finish with a piece of contemporary dialect speech from a *young* speaker. In the past, it is always older, not to say, ancient, speakers who have been recorded (see, for example, SED's declared policy quoted in Chapter 4, section "Subject Areas", sub-section "Introduction"), but we feel it is of interest to know the state of the dialect as it is today among a younger generation. (Inevitably, having decided against using the International Phonetic Alphabet, much of the vowel quality of Mrs. Rogers's speech is lost, but, in fact, the orthography employed by the nineteenth century editors is really no better, suffering from considerable uncertainty as to precisely what quality of vowel or diphthong is intended.)

It should also be noted that, apart from individual responses, SED made lengthy transcripts of their informants' speech and these – since the recent Government cutbacks closed Leeds University's Institute of Dialect and Folk Life Studies – are now in the care of Professor T. A. Shippey of the University of Birmingham (see also Chapter 1, note 17).

As a postscript, it may be of interest to quote Dartnell and Goddard's gloomy prognostication of 1892: "The use of the dialect would appear gradually to be dying out now in the county, thanks, perhaps, to the spread of education which too often renders the rustic half-ashamed of his native tongue ... Every year is likely to add to the difficulty of collecting, and if it is not done now, the task may soon become a hopeless one" (*WAM* (1892)). Thanks largely to the efforts of D&G, and more recently, of SED, we may say that the job of collecting has been fairly thoroughly done, but if "the use of dialect appeared to be dying out in the county" in 1892, the rate of disappearance since then has greatly accelerated to the extent that the dialect now, at least as far as the lexicon is concerned, appears to us, to be bordering on extinction among younger speakers. Together with education, in more recent decades it has been above all the influence and prestige status of radio and television, which – until very recently, at least – have purveyed a fairly uniform Standard English, that have contributed to the steady decline of the dialect.

The King & Qveenes Entertainement (1636). (edited by Bang and Brotanek, 1903)

(... the country dance might be introduc'd by some

Clounes speaking; And because most of the Interlocutors were Wilshire men, that country Dialect was chosen . . .)

Tom O Wilkin, you come a day after the vaire[1], shud ha come zooner, man. Welcome Maull, Mastris Queene, you dont know who this Wilkin, or who this Maull is, chill[2] tell you. These twaine were vengeance[3] in love one with other, as might be my zell and Madge for all the world. Maull here had a very pestlence[3] woman to her mother, as might be Madges Dame, you know, Madge, your Dame is a very veirce woman . . . Now that Mother being a pestlence woman as I sed before, wood by no meanes possible that these twaine loving wretches shud be man and wife together, cause Wilkin had not zheepe enough vorzooth, vor that mother was damnation[3] covetous: Yet for all that Maull being a parlous[4] wench as you zee, stole from her mother, and clapt up the match betweene um, her mother being as ingrant[5] of it as you are. Now all the parish wondred why she shud be led into a vooles paradise by him, you zee there are them in place be as proper as him zell every inch, but when all came to all, she zed she was led away with his singing vorzooth. Now to zay troth he zings well, though hee bee nothing comparable to the Munstrell, that zung the zong of "Short-coate" when you were here last, vor all that, you shall heare him zing a 'bomination[3] vyne zong of his love to Maull. Zing Wilkin, weele get leave to stay zo long: What che thinke thou wants a Viddle, chill vetch thee a Viddle, man, if there be a Viddle in the house. [He goes in, and brings out a Theorbo.[6]] Che can borrow no Viddle but this, and heres one aumost as long as a May-pole; prithee make zhift for once.

(lines 220–59)

Extracts from the genuine remains of William Little (early 19th century) (published in Akerman, J. Y. 1853. *Wiltshire tales*)

STOOPID OWLD WOSBIRD

I've allus bin as vlush o' money as a twoad is o' veathers;[1] but, if ever I gets rich, I'll put it ael in Ziszeter[2] bank, and not do as owld Smith, the miller, did, comin whoam vrom market one nite. Martal[3] avraid o' thieves a was, zo a puts his pound-bills and ael th'money a'd a got about un, in a hole in the wall, and the next marnin a couldn't remember whereabouts twas, and had to pull purty[4] nigh a mile o' wall down before a could vind it. Stoopid owld wosbird[5]!

OWLD POPLE

"How far d'e cal't to Zirencester, my friend?" zays a Cockney genelman one day to owld Pople, as a wor breakin stwones[1] on th' road. "Dwont[1] kneow zich a please," zays he, scrattin's yeard,[2] "never yead[2] on't avore!" – "What!" zays the genelman, "never heard o' Zirencester?" – "Noa", zays he, "I aint." – "Why, it's the next town." "Haw! haw!" zays Pople; "you means Ziszeter; why didn't e zay so? it's about vower mile off." – He was a rum owld customer, thuck[3] owld Pople. One day zomebody axed[4] un how var't was to Ziszeter. "Ho! dree[5] miles this weather." (It was nation[6] dirty and slippy.) "Why so?" said the man to'n; "Ho, it's about two miles in vine weather; but when it's hocksey,[7] like this, we allows[8] a mile vor zlippin back!"

Passages appended to Dartnell and Goddard's glossary (1893)

PUTTEN UP THE BANNS
(contributed by Edward Slow, South Wiltshire)
Wen Zal Slatter coorteed Jim Bleak he wur under-carter, an she wur maid a ael wuk up at Hill Varm. Zoo thay greed ta putt up tha banns unbeknown to their measter an missus. Wen Varmer comed[1] out a chirch thic[2] Zundy a gooes straight inta kitchen wur Zal wur cookin a gurt[3] laig[4] a

168

mutten var dinner, an a zaays, "Zal," a zaays, "Wur that thee an Jim I yeard[5] caal'd whoam[6] bit[7] now?" "I specs twur,[8] measter," zaays Zal. "Why, wat in tha wordle[9] diss[10] thee want ta get married var? Hassen[11] 'ee got a good whoam,[6], a good bade[12] ta sleep on? an a good laig a mutten ta zet down to wen bist ungry?" "O eece,[13] measter," zaays Zal, "I knaas ael that, bit did 'ee ever know a wench as hooden[14] gie up a laig o' mutten var a whole man?"

THE CANNINGS VAWK
(contributed by E. H. Goddard, North Wiltshire)
I niver wur at Cannins but once as I knaws[2] on, an that wur when Mr. Jones wur alive. I went awver wi he to Cannins Veast. I mind thur wur a lot o em thur from Caan as wur a tellin up zuch tales as was never about the Cannins vawk.[1]

The' telled I as zome on em got up the Church tower, and dunged[3] that thur – what is it? – atop o' the tower, to make un grow as big as the spire. I never he-ard tell o' zuch a thing! Should 'ee iver thenk as twer true?

An the' telled[4] I as twernt[5] but a vurry veow years ago as zome on em hired[6] as ther wur a comut[7] ur what 'ee caals ut, to be zeed in 'Vize market-place, an pretty nigh aal Cannins went in thur to zee un, an niver thought o' lookin to zee wur they cudden zee un at whoam.[8] What some girt[9] stups[10] they must a bin!

An thur wur a cooper ur zummat o' that, as cudden putt th'yead[11] into a barr'l; an a telled he's bwoy[12] to get inside and howld un[13] up till he'd a vastened un. An when a done the bwoy[13] hollered out droo[14] the bung hawl, "How be I to get out, veyther?" – That bit tickled I, bless 'ee! moor'n aal on't!

Arterwards one on em axed[15] I if thur wurden[16] a Cannins girl in sarvice at our place; an I zes "I blieve as tes." An a zes, "Do 'ee iver zaa *Baa*! to she?"[17] An I zes "Noa, vur why should I zaay *Baa*! to she?"[17] An a zes "You should allus zaay *Baa*! to a body as[18] comes vrom Cannins." "Wull," I zes, "I shudden like to zaay *Baa*! to any body wi'out I

169

knowed[19] the rason ont." An then a telled I as the' had a tidd-
lin lamb as wur terble dickey,[20] an the' putt un into th'o-ven,
to kip un warm an shut un in an forgot aal about un, an lef un
in thur. An when the' awpened the o-ven agean a wur raws-
ted droo![14] – Wull, I come whoam,[8] an niver thought nothen
more on't fur a lenth o' time, till one daay as I wur a-workin
in the garden, measter an missus wur out, an the girls come
out an begun a 'oondermentin[20] an terrifyin I. An aal at once
this yer[21] shot into my mind, an I looks[22] up at the cook an I
zes,[22] "*Baa!*" But her didden take no nautice, an a went on
chatterin. An I zes "*Baa!*" agean. An that put her pot on,[23]
bless 'ee! at a terrible rate, an she zes to I, "Who be *you*" –
she zes, – "to zaay *Baa!* to I?" An wi that they both on em
went auf in-a-doors, an they niver come a-meddlin wi I[24]
agean fur a long whiles.

Twentieth-century folk tales

SAVING THE DUCK FROM DROWNING
(from Williams A. (1913) *Villages of the White Horse* 13.
East Wiltshire dialect.)
"Le's see, tha's wher tha dunged tha monniment, to make e'
grow, down Churl way, un' it?"

"Naw tha didn't, neether. Tha dunged the staple, tha did,
at B'kampton, to make un[2] graw as 'igh as tha tower."

"An' wher was it as tha whitewashed tha owl' rawn
bool?"[3]

"Aw, that was Lavinton way. Didn' we ust to tarment[4] ole
Jakey 'bout 'e! Us[5] got un as wi-yuld!"[6]

"An' that yent[7] so bad as gettin' in tha pond, to save the
owl' duck from drowndin'.[8] Tha's right anuf, yun[7] it?"

"Aw, aa, cos I wur ther an' the best o't wur, a put 'is best
claws[9] an to do't wi'! Tha ole chap wur terr'ble frade tha duck
ood[10] be drownded,[8] an' 'gun[11] gettin' in aater 'n.[2] Then Billy
'Edger, the old cyarter,[7] comes up an' ses: 'I should go an'
put mi best claws[9] on vust,[12] Willum, if I was in thy place.'
An' baggar if a didn't go an' do't, too, an zaved[13] tha ole

170

duck. But thee[5] musten't saay nothin' about it ther now, yels[7] thee't soon get chocked out[14] on't[15]."

THE RESHIT

(Told by Joe Garlick and published in Tanner H., and Tanner R. (1939) *A Wiltshire village* 174)

I can moind when I wur up at Whoam[1] Varm, us[2] dursn't[3] go noigh thic[4] stavel[5] barn noights for the reshit as[6] did[7] wallop and bump on thic drashing[8] vloor.[9] Ah, and 'twurnt on'y in the barn, noither: a did get in thic byre and tie they hosses' manes all in gurt[10] knots-loike,[11] so as us wur fair put to it ta onloosen of 'em. Us did make the lock fast noights, but thic reshit must a crope[12] drough[8] the keyhole or leastways down in under the door, an' come marnin'[13] they was all a-twisted[14] up zame[15] as avore.[9] Varmer[9] wur in a vair[9] caddle.[5] Fust when us telled[12] un what we seen, a thowt us'd 'ad a drop too much tiddly.[5] "Thee ca'sn't zee so well as thee cou'st, ca'st?"[16] a says, nasty-loike.[11]

Then when a zeed[12] for hissen[17] a kep' a-broibin'[14] o' we[2] and says as us done[12] it; then a did[7] twit us as us was aveard[9] to go past the barken[5] arter dark. Wull, it come so's I couldn't aboide it no longer, and one noight I says[3] as I 'ud go up thic varm fur to watch for they ghostieses.[18] I 'adn't but just come out the drung[5] between Laweses's[18] housen[19] and ourn[17] when I sees[3] Will Clapp.

"Wur bist thee gwine,[1] you?"[20] a says. I tells[3] un[21] and a says, "Thee best boide wur thee bist, Joe." Howsumdever,[22] a zees as I wur set on't and a comes along of[23] I. Us wurn't no more'n a lug[5] from thic barn when us heared[12] zummat[15]. "'E be the reshit!" I says. "Do zound loike a main[5] vew[9] on[24] 'em," a says. "Awpen thic thur geat and get atop of thic thur mixen[5], Joe," a says, "and peek in at un.[21]" I never heared sich a rumpus as come[12] then: 'twur loike as if zomebody[15] wur drashing[8] with a 'nation[5] gurt[10] drashel.[8] Me swallow[5] wur as dry as a gix,[25] and Will 'e wur all of a shiver, but anyways a crope[12] up the mixen and I did climb up atop of 'e[21] . . .

171

But I never seed[12] nowt.

No, and nobody never zeed nowt, neither. Volks[9] as[6] never heared[12] un[21] did[7] say as thiccun wurn't no reshit, and thur wurn't narn.[26] Zum di[7] zay as 'twur Old Nick hissen.[17] I 'ouldn't[27] loike fur to zay as 'twur ... And then, I 'ouldn't loike fur to zay as 'twurn't.

Transcripts of a tape-recording of Mrs Rose Rogers (aged 28, Pewsey, May 1984)

THE PROPRIETOR

Oh, I mus tell you a funny thing bout wh'n I worked in the paper-shop. We ad[1] quoite a good larrf[2] down there. There was a chap in who asked me if the proprietor – I ope I've pronounced that right – was in, so I looked a' im an I said, "Is it ordered?" And he said, "No". So I wen along an I looked at the books[3] on the counter and I said, "You sure it's not ordered?" an 'e said, "Yes, definitely." I said, "Well, we aven't got one on the counter an we aven't got one ordered, so I'm fraid you carn have one." An 'e looked at me an 'e said, "I think we've got our loines crossed somewhere". An I said, "No," I said, "If it's not ordered we aven't got one," An he said, "No, I'm referring to Mr. Flippence." "Oh," I said, "I thought it was a magazine for a minute", an I never forget that, I honestly thought 'the proprietor' was a book![3]

WILFIE'S DEAD

One Christmas 'e came up when my eldest[1] brother was very ..., well, 'e was bout three or four, so I can remember Dad comin up Christmas Eve on the pushbike, an e ad four rabbits on the back bike, y' see, all dead they were – I a spec tha's wha' 'e got from poachin somewhere – an Gillo said 'e come up High Street an – y' know the light on Ball Corner? – he wen three times round that larmp[2] an then Gillo di' say[3] 'e jus clapsed in a heap on the road an is bike an 'e led[4] there, an 'e kep sayin, "Poor Wilfie, poor Wilfie, poor Wilfie's dead." Well, we ad a ..., Dad ad a nephew long Easterton

172

Lane called Wilfie Head, an my mum come[5] out an thought, "Oh my God, Wilfie 'Ead's dead!" So she wen along, come rushin along Easterton Lane to find out, an Aunie Rose said, "No, wha' y'on about?", said "Wilf's alright." That's what my dad used to call rabbits – "wilfies". Don' ask me whoy![6] ... All these damn rabbits ung on the bike were stone dead an there was my dad: "Poor Wilfie's dead." Gillo said, "I c'n see him now led[4] there in a heap, he wen three times roun the light an then – CRASH!

Commentary

THE KING & QVEENES ENTERTAINEMENT
The German editors remark that the dialect in this antimasque is notable for being far more authentic than the stock stage dialect used in most sixteenth and seventeenth century plays.

1 *you come a day after the fair* (idiom), i.e. you come too late.
2 *chill*; *che*; Forms of *I will* (a contraction of *che will*) and *I*. (compare p. 16)
3 *vengeance in love*; *a very pestlence woman*; *damnation covetous*; *a 'bomination vyne zong* A syntactical peculiarity; the use of a noun where an adverb is required. Note that D&G record the third usage in the clipped form, *nation*, and that it appears in extract "Owld Pople".
4 *parlous* Here meaning "clever, cunning, mischievous".
5 *ingrant* A "comic" perversion of *ignorant*.
6 *Theorbo* A large double-necked lute with two sets of strings.

EXTRACTS FROM THE GENUINE REMAINS OF WILLIAM LITTLE
These passages exemplify, according to D&G 205, "the North Wilts. speech of some fifty or sixty years ago." [i.e. of the 1830's]. They may, however, be considered to reflect the dialect of the early nineteenth century, as William Little, a North Wiltshire shepherd, was already an old man when Akerman was a boy.

Stoopid Owld Wosbird
1 *as flush of money as a toad is of feathers* A nice dialect simile! and also a pun only possible in dialect, where *flush*, apparently a separate word of different etymology from *flush* meaning "well supplied with money", also means "fledged", as found by SED, which also records the *w* glide in *toad*. The toad's featherless state is stressed in the late-twelfth cen-

tury *Descriptio Norfolciensium*, line 196. The proverb, "You can't get feathers off a frog", is discussed in *Notes and queries* 4th series, vol. 11 (1873), pp. 63, 352.

2 *Ziszeter* see extract "Owld Pople".
3 *martal* i.e. mortally.
4 *purty* i.e. *pretty* (see p. 23).
5 *wosbird* OED cites Thomas Hardy's *Tess of the d'Urbervilles* cap.xxi: "Jack Dollop, a 'hor's-bird of a fellow." Hardy's spelling shows his awareness of the word's etymology from *whore's bird* i.e. "bastard", where "bird" = OED *bird* l.c. meaning "child".

Owld Pople

1 *stwones*; *Dwont* For the *w* glide see p. 21.
2 *yead*; *yeard* For the phonology of this, see the *y* glide, p. 21.
3 *thuck* See p. 28.
4 *axed* i.e. *aksed* for "asked" For such metathesis see p. 23.
5 *dree* i.e. *three* For this phonological change, see p. 18.
6 *nation* See note 3. to extract "The King & Qveenes Entertainement".
7 *hocksey* i.e. "muddy, miry" from OE *horx, horsc, foul, dirty,* + (later) adjectival *-y* termination (see Chapter 2). The base of this dialect "double" adjective is OE *horu, filth, dirt,* found as the first element of the place-name *Hor*ton, near Devizes.
8 *we allows* For similar lack of grammatical concord, see p. 32.

Putten up the Banns

1 *comed* see p. 34.
2 *thic* see p. 28.
3 *gurt* i.e. *great* (see p. 23).
4 *laig* For the diphthong see p. 20.
5 *yead* See note 2 to extract 'Owld Pople'.
6 *whoam* i.e. *home* (see p. 21).
7 *bit* i.e. *but*
8 *twur* i.e. *it were*, showing lack of grammatical concord, see pp. 32, 35.
9 *wordle* a metathesised form of *world*, (see p. 23).
10 *diss thee* i.e. *dost thou.* See pp. 26 and 37.
11 *hassen 'ee* for **hastn't thee* i.e. *hast thou not.*
12 *bade* (pronounced, "bayed") for *bed*, shows similar diphthongisation to that noted in n.4.
13 *eece* i.e. *yes* For loss of initial *y-* sound, see p. 21.
14 *hooden* i.e. *wouldn't*, a phonological development in two stages: 1. loss of initial *w-* (see p. 21); 2. hypercorrection, as if 'restoring' a dropped *h-* (see p. 22).

The Cannings Vawk

Katherine Briggs writes: "A particularly large class [of Jocular Tale] in England . . . is the Local Taunt, the Noodle Tale multiplied to cover a whole village. Gotham, whether in Nottingham or Sussex, is generally taken as the typical village of fools, though over 50 places can be found scattered through the different counties of England against whom the same sort of accusations are levelled. One of the commonest taunts is that they tried to wall in the cuckoo" [see chapter 8] (Briggs, K. M. 1977 *British folk tales and legend: a sampler*:51). In our county, it is Bishops Cannings that has acquired the doubtful distinction of being the Noodle Village par excellence, and Goddard's composition gives four such stories; interestingly, the last story is now generally current in the updated *Pet/Baby-in-the-Microwave* version. (For a recent study on this motif see Brunvand, J. H. 1983. *The vanishing hitch-hiker: urban legends and their meaning*. Picador ed. 56–61, 63–4. There is evidence from the Anglo-Saxon era, not known to Brunvand, that some mothers were in the habit of placing their children in ovens in the belief that it cured fever, see Haddan, H. W. & Stubbs, W. 1964 *Councils and ecclesiastical documents* 3 : 190)

See further: Stern, J. L. 1977. "Blason Populaire or Have you heard about the folks from . . . ?" *Wiltshire Folklife* 1.ii.5–7, and Bigger, S. F. 1977 "Those 'Idiot villages' again", *Wiltshire folklife* 1.iii.21–4. For comparative evidence from just south of the Wiltshire border, see Rawlence, E. A. 1915, "Some old village jokes and games which obtained in the Blackmore Vale in the last century", *Proceedings of the Dorset Natural History and Antiquarian Field Club*, 36: 6–15.

1 *vawk* i.e. *folk*.
2 *I knaws* i.e. *I know* showing lack of grammatical concord, see p. 32.
3 *dunged* i.e. spread with manure.
4 *telled* showing weak past tense for StE strong past *told* (see p. 33).
5 *twernt* i.e. *it weren't*, showing lack of grammatical concord, see p. 32).
6 *hired* i.e. *heard*.
7 *comut* i.e. *comet*.
8 *whoam* i.e. *home* (see p. 21).
9 *girt* i.e. *great* (see p. 23).
10 *stups* i.e. "stupid people".
11 *th'yead* i.e. *the head* (the flat end of a barrel). See note 2 to extract "Owld Pople".
12 *bwoy* For the *w* glide, see p. 21.
13 *un* i.e. *'n*, see p. 27.
14 *droo* i.e. *through* For this phonological change, see p. 18.
15 *axed* see note 4 to Owld Pople.

16 *wurden'* i.e. *weren'(t)* with inorganic *d* (see p. 50).
17 *to she* for StE *to her* (see p. 27).
18 *as* for StE *who* or *that* (see p. 29).
19 *knowed* showing weak past tense for StE strong past *knew* (see p. 33).
20 *'oondermentin* for *wondermenting* i.e. "playing the fool, wasting time over unprofitable work" (D&G), showing an interesting formation of a verb from a noun and loss of initial w- (see p. 21).
21 *yer* i.e. *here*, see note 2 to extract "Owld Pople".
22 *I looks*; *I says*, see note 2 above.
23 *put her pot on* a nice idiom, i.e. "got her goat".
24 *I* for StE *me*, as throughout (see p. 26).

TWENTIETH CENTURY FOLK TALES
Saving the duck from drowning
Three more Local Taunts: the Cherhill Monument is near Devizes. Katherine Briggs notes that "The accusation of manuring the church to make it grow is one very commonly employed in local taunts in England, but has not a motif-number." In Wiltshire, this Noodle Tale motif is more usually attributed to nearby Bishop's Cannings rather than Beckhampton, see the first anecdote under the Text, "Cannings Vawk" above. Painting an animal some more desirable colour is also a popular motif in this sort of tale. The main Noodle Tale here is the well-known Motif number J.1909.7 "Fear that frog (or duck) may drown".

1 *un* for *isn't*.
2 *un* i.e. *'n* for StE *him*, see p. 27; *thee* for *thou*, now StE *you*, see p. 26.
3 *rawn bool* for *roan bull*.
4 *tarment*; see "Vowels", p. 20.
5 *us* for *we*; see "Pronouns; personal", p. 26.
6 i.e. two syllables, as often in StE too.
7 *yent* i.e. *ent*, *ain't* for StE *isn't* (also *yun*); *yels* i.e. *else*; *cyarter* i.e. *carter*; all showing the *y-* glide, see p. 21.
8 *drowndin'* i.e. *drowning*, showing intrusive -*d*-, see p. 50.
9 *claws* i.e. *clothes*.
10 *ood* for *would*, showing loss of intial *w*-, see p. 21.
11 *'gun* for *begun*.
12 *vust* for *first*, showing dialect initial *v*- for StE *f*-.
13 *zaved* for *saved*, showing dialect initial *z*- for StE *s*-.
14 *chocked out* for *chucked out* (colloquial).
15 *on* for *of*, see n. 24 to Text "The Reshit".

TWENTIETH CENTURY FOLKTALES
The Reshit

176

Katherine Briggs has classified this tale as an example of Motif No. F.473.5 "Poltergeist makes noises" (v. *Dictionary of British folktales and legends* 35), though the details of this local demon's behaviour are not clear, nor is the etymology of its name. At first sight, from the context, it might be conjectured that the name of this demon (not recorded elsewhere to our knowledge, e.g. not in OED or EDD) is connected with the word *thresh*, but we should regularly expect *drash* or *draish* in Wiltshire dialect (see p. 18, nor does there seem to be any precedent for loss of initial *th*. There is a hint in the tale that the reshit need not necessarily be a solitary demon: might there perhaps be some connexion with *ra(t)chet* (variant of *rache*), a hunting-dog, and more significantly, when led by the archangel Gabriel, the name of the hounds of the Wild Hunt (see OED under *rache, ratch* sb[1] and *Gabriel-rache(t)*)? John Jamieson in his *An etymological dictionary of the Scottish language* (1808) records from Lanarkshire a demon whose name is a corruption of the latter *Gabriel* form, *Gaubertie*-shells, which he defines thus: "a hobgoblin who . . . has been heard to make a loud roaring, accompanied with a barking similar to that of little dogs . . ." (In the late 15th century, *Gabrielle rache* is glossed *camalion*, which should normally mean "giraffe" at this period, but it is difficult to believe it can mean that here. cf. OED under *camelion*.) However, it must be admitted that this tale, at least, shows no vestigial traces of canine characteristics in the reshit's behaviour, and its etymology must remain uncertain.

The other well-known folklore motif occurring in this tale, is F.473.4.1 "Spirit rides horses and mules at night". Such "elf-locks", as tangled or matted curls of hair in horse-manes etc., were called, were supposed to be made by elves, fairies or witches riding the horses at night. (The classic reference to this belief in English is in Shakespeare's *Romeo and Juliet* I.iv.89–90.) The Wiltshire antiquary, John Aubrey, in his *Miscellanies* (1696), recommends the already old, traditional remedy to avert this mishap, of hanging a self-bored stone above the stalls.

1 *whoam*; *gwine*; for *home*; *going*; showing the *w* glide (see p. 21).
2 *us* for *we*; *we* for *us*; see "Pronouns: personal", p. 26.
3 *dursn't* i.e. the old 2nd person singular form of *dare* (StE would need the 1st person plural form *daren't* here). See further Chapter 3, note 7. Note the similar lack of concord in *I says, I sees*, etc.
4 *thic* for *that*, see "Pronouns: demonstrative", p. 28.
5 *stavel barn* i.e. a barn resting on staddle-stones, raised off the ground to protect its contents from damp and vermin. *caddle*, i.e. confusion (D&G). *tiddly* i.e. *alcoholic liquor*. *barken* i.e. *farmyard*, see Chapter 4, sub-section "The farm and farm-life". *drung*, i.e. *alley*. *lug*, i.e. the linear measurement formerly known as a *rod, pole or perch*. *main*, i.e. very; *mixen*, i.e. *dungheap*. *'nation*, see n. 3 to Text "The King and

177

Qveenes Entertainement". *swallow*, i.e. *throat*.

6 *as* for *that*, see p. 29.

7 *did wallop*; *did twit*; *did climb*; periphrastic past tenses where StE would use the simple past, see p. 36.

8 *drough* for *through*; *drash* for *thresh*; *drashel* for *threshel*, i.e. *flail*, etc., showing dialect initial *dr-* for StE *thr-*.

9 *aveard* for *afeared*, StE *afraid*; *avore* for *before*; *vloor* for *floor*; *varm(er)* for *farm(er)*; *vair* for *fair*; *vew* for *few*, etc., showing dialect (initial) *v-* for *f-*.

10 *gurt* for *great*, showing metathesis caused by the strong quality of the SW *r*, see p. 23, and compare n. 25 below.

11 *-loike*; a frequent general English dialect and colloquial usage, see OED *like* adv.B.7 "used parenthetically to qualify a preceding statement = 'as it were', 'so to speak'."

12 *crope* for *crept*; *telled* for *told*; *done* for *did*; *seed, zeed* for *saw*; *heared* for *heard*, *come* for *came*; for similar irregular past tense forms, see pp. 33, 34.

13 *marnin'*, see "Vowels", p. 20.

14 *a-twisted*; *a-broibin'* (i.e. *taunting*); see "Participles", p. 33.

15 *zomebody*; *zame*; *zummat*; *zound*; showing dialect initial *z-* for *s-*.

16 "Thee ca'sn't zee so well as thee cou'st, ca'st?" A well-known dialect cliché, often trotted out as an example of dialect.

17 *hissen* for *himself*, not a form recorded by SED, which found *hisself*, see "Prepositions; reflexive", p. 28; *ourn* for *ours*, see "Prepositions: possessive".

18 *ghostieses* and *Laweses*; double plurals, see p. 25.

19 *housen*; archaic plural, see p. 25.

20 *you*, see "Pronouns: disjunctive", p. 29.

21 *un*, i.e. *'n*, for StE *him*, see p. 27; *'e* for *him*.

22 *howsumdever* showing inorganic *-d-*, see p. 50.

23 *along of*; a double preposition, see "Prepositions", p. 31.

24 *on* for *of*, see "Prepositions", p. 32.

25 *dry as a gix*, a dialect simile, see p. 150.

26 *narn* for *none*, showing unhistorical *r*-colouring, see p. 22.

27 *'ouldn't* for *wouldn't*, showing loss of initial *w-*, see p. 21.

TRANSCRIPTS OF TAPE-RECORDING OF MRS ROGERS

Mrs Rogers's dialect does not show the voicing of initial $\theta \rightarrow \eth$, one of the characteristics of the South-Western dialects: this suggests that the phonological boundary, at least, has shifted further west since SED's recording, though, doubtless, amongst the *younger* people even then, it was already receding westwards. It should be noted that the orthography we are using for the most part masks the distinctive quality of the vowel sounds. It is noticeable, too, both in these passages and in completely informal conversation, that Mrs. Rogers employs very little of the dialect lexicon available to earlier generations of speakers (compare the evidence of SED and the nineteenth century passages).

The Proprietor
1 *ad* i.e. *had* showing dropped *h*-, as throughout.
2 *larrf* showing *r*-colouring in a word with no historical *r*, see p. 22.
3 *books* for *magazines* (see below), a common colloquial usage.

Wilfie's Dead
1 *eldest* Note correct specialised form of the superlative where many StE speakers might use *oldest*.
2 *larmp* showing *r*-colouring in a word with no historical *r*, see p. 22.
3 *di' say* i.e. *did say*, the periphrastic past tense where StE would use *said*.
4 *led* for *laid* i.e. StE *lay*. This is a common confusion, general in dialect and colloquial English, between the past tense of *lay* (meaning *set down*) i.e. *laid*, and the past tense of *lie* (meaning *be prone*) i.e. *lay*.
5 *come* showing weak past tense for StE strong pst *came* (see p. 34).
6 *Wilfies* Don't ask us why either! It may simply be that *wilfie* is an affectionate nickname for *rabbit*, just like the names *neddy*, *cuddy* and *donkey* itself (discussed in Chapter 4).

Appendix 4

THE CHILD'S LEXICON

Introduction

The "children's dialect questionnaire" which follows
been adapted, with permission, from Iona and Peter Op
The lore and language of school children (1959).
questionnaire may be further adapted to the requiremen
particular school situations; an example of a simplified
sion, used with junior school children, is given at the en

When conducting the questionnaire, it is important
the children should not feel in any way intimidated
should be emphasised that it is not a test and there a
right and wrong answers (only irrelevant ones, whic
hope you will do your best to obviate, rephrasing our fo
lations wherever necessary). Because some questions
on sensitive areas such as nicknames for teachers, and c
will be bound to elicit vocabulary of varying degrees c
garity, we feel that the best responses will be obtained
atmosphere of anonymity. We have frequently sug;
well-known examples of particular types of saying, r
etc., and it will often be essential to prompt childre
these.

Teachers may wish to use this questionnaire as a
board for wider language investigations (children's
ground and singing games for example) or for work in
areas of the curriculum. Collaborative projects, invo

181

comparison of responses from children at schools in different parts of the county, may be particularly rewarding.

A children's dialect questionnaire

1.00 Write down any nonsense rhymes you know (for example, "Mrs. White had a fright..."; "One fine day in the middle of the night...").

2.00 Write down any rhymes you know for ball bouncing or skipping.

3.00 Chase games:

3.01 If you are playing a chase game, what do you call the person who is the chaser?

3.02 How do you decide who is to be the chaser? (If you use a special rhyme write it down.)

3.03 What do you call this type of choosing someone with this type of rhyme?

4.00 Write down any tongue-twisters you know (for example, "How much wood could..."; "She sells..."; "Peter Piper...").

5.00 Sometimes people ask too many questions! (perhaps you have a younger brother or sister who annoys you like this, or one friend in particular). Sometimes it can get too much and you are tempted to give the questioner a "clever" or cheeky answer back (for example, if someone asked you "Where are you going?" you might reply, "There and back to see how far it is!"). Do you know or use any such clever replies to any of the following questions? (Write down the question and your smart answer):

5.01 Where've you been?

5.02 Who were you with?

5.03 Why?

5.04 What for?

5.05 What's the time?

5.06 How old are you?

5.07 Where are you going?

5.08 (D'you know) what?
And, in the same way, how might you reply to someone who says:

5.09 "Hey!" or

5.10 "Eh?"

6.00 As well as annoying questions, people do annoying
things! What would you say to a friend who did each
of the following things (Write down your "clever"
remark, if you know one, together with the annoying
thing):

6.01 got in your light

6.02 left the door open

6.03 pushed in front of you

6.04 kept asking you to get things for him/her

6.05 talked too much

6.06 had buttons or zips undone

6.07 was very impatient

6.08 said "I'm telling"

6.09 said "I don't care"

6.10 told you a piece of news that you'd all known for ages

6.11 told you a joke that everyone had heard already

7.00 What might you shout at a friend on a bicycle or at
someone in the street who you think looks funny?

8.00 Describe any tricks you know for catching your
friends out (for example, "Do you collect stamps?"
or the rhyme which begins "Adam and Eve
and..." or "Are you a P.L.P.?" or "Made you
look!" or any trick bets (for example, "I can jump
higher than a house") or trick spellings (for example,
"Constantinople is a long word, how do you spell
it?").

9.00 Write down any riddles you know. Do you know any
funny versions of Christmas carols? Do you know
any rhymes about film or T.V. stars or the Prime
Minister?

10.00 If you told your friends a secret, how would you
make them swear to keep it? Write down the words

183

they would have to say and any special action they would have to make.

10.01   What happens to people if they tell a sworn secret?

10.02   If you swop something with a friend what do you say to make sure the swop will be for good? Is there anything you do as well?

10.03   If something is offered to a group of you, what do you have to shout to make sure you get it?

10.04   If you find something you'd like to keep, what do you say?

10.05   If one of you is going to have to do something that none of you like doing, what do you shout to make sure it isn't you?

10.06   If you're playing a chase game and want to have a moment's rest for some reason, what is the word you have to say and what is the action or sign you have to make?

11.00   Write down any nicknames you use for people of your own age who you don't like, or for friends who are very greedy, or who are always late or last.

12.00   Do you have your own words for your mouth, stomach, feet, hands, toes, fingers (especially your little fingers), nose, ears, face.

13.00   Do you have your own words for certain animals, birds and insects (for example, dog, cat, sparrow, blackbird, owl, wasp, bee, spider, ladybird, dragonfly, etc.).

14.00   Give the names you call each of the following types of person:

14.01   a spoil-sport

14.02   someone who thinks he/she is clever

14.03   someone who is grumpy

14.04   someone who is silly

14.05   someone who is nosey

14.06   someone who boasts

14.07   someone who copies

14.08   someone who stares

14.09	someone who cries a lot
14.10	someone who tells tales
14.11	someone who is the teacher's favourite
14.12	someone who is a coward
14.13	someone who is "posh"
15.00	How do you tell someone you don't like: to go away? to be quiet? How would you punish someone none of you liked or who had got you all into trouble?
16.00	What magic practices do you know? What do you say or do to make sure you have good luck or keep away back luck? Is there anything you must say or do if you see:
16.01	a white horse
16.02	a black cat
16.03	a white cat
16.04	a hare
16.05	a rabbit
16.06	a dog (any particular colour?)
16.07	a cuckoo
16.08	a crow
16.09	a magpie
16.10	a beetle
16.11	a spider
16.12	an ambulance
16.13	a rainbow
	What if you hear:
16.14	a dog howl
16.15	an owl screech?
	Do you have any belief about:
16.16	Breaking a mirror
16.17	Catching a leaf
16.18	Treading on cracks in the pavement
16.19	Walking under a ladder
16.20	Walking over a bridge
	What must you say or do if you find:
16.21	a button

16.22   a cigarette packet or match-box

16.23   a four-leaf clover

16.24   a coin

16.25   a lump of coal

16.26   a feather

16.27   a horseshoe

16.28   a needle or a pin

16.29   a specially shaped or coloured stone (specify)

16.30   a knife

16.31   a dropped flower

16.32   Is there anything you must do or say to bring you good luck in exams, or tests, in games, or to give you courage?

17.00   Describe what sort of things you do (if anything!) on the following "special" days:

17.01   Shrove Tuesday

17.02   Mother's Day

17.03   Valentine's Day

17.04   Ash Wednesday

17.05   May Day

17.06   April Fool's Day

17.07   New Year's Eve and Day

17.08   Hallowe'en

17.09   Guy Fawkes Day

17.10   Oak Apple Day (May 29th)

18.00   If a new boy or girl arrives at your school, what kind of tricks do you play on them? Do you have a nick-name for new boys or girls?

19.00   What tricks do you play on the first day of the month?

20.00   What things do you do at school:

20.01   on a person's birthday

20.02   when someone arrives in new clothes

20.03   if you lose a tooth

21.00   What do you say if you say the same thing at exactly the same time as someone else?

22.00   Do you know any cure for warts?

23.00   Do you know any secret language that you and your friends can talk in so that nobody else listening can understand? Explain how it works

24.00   Friends:

24.01   What is your name for a close friend of the same sex as you?

24.02   When you make a new friend or break up with an old friend, do you have any special things you say and do?

24.03   What is your opinion of boys in general?

24.04   What is your opinion of girls in general?

24.05   How do you know if a boy has girlfriends or if a girl has boyfriends?

24.06   How can you find out if you will marry and who you will marry?

24.07   What signs do you believe show that a boy/girl you like, likes you (for example, ears burning, tripping up stairs).

25.00   How can you find out what you will do when you grow up?

26.00   What ways of fortune telling do you know?

27.00   Do you make special toys out of paper that you work with both hands from which your friends have to choose a number, then a colour, etc.? What do you call these paper toys?
        What things do you write on the inside? Make one!

28.00   Do you have any special nicknames for children from other villages, towns or other schools? Write down any such names or rhymes.

29.00   Describe a trick you or your friends have played on a teacher. Write down any nicknames or rhymes you have for your teachers. Give examples of your teachers' jokes or any of their clever answers! (for example, in reply to someone who says "The bell has gone!")

30.00   If someone who is not ill takes the day off school without telling parents or teachers what is this called?

31.00 Do you have any nicknames or rhymes about police-
men?

31.01 If you are doing something naughty and one of you is
keeping a lookout, what do you say he/she is doing?

31.02 If someone got caught but the rest of you got away,
what would you say to comfort him/her?

An example of a simplified questionnaire for school use

This questionnaire was adapted by Mr D. Hollings for use
with Junior children at Pewsey Vale School.

1 What do you say about someone who stays off school
when they are perfectly well?

2 What if someone arrives at school, but sneaks off during
the day?

3 If you told someone a secret, how would you get them to
promise to keep it?

4 If you've done something wrong and someone tells of you
to the teacher, what do you say about them?

5 If you are in a group and you want to claim or reserve a
special place, what do you say?
For example, in York, kids say "Foggie I go first"

6 At primary school, if you played a chasing game, what
did you call the game?

7 What do you call the person doing the chasing?

8 What ways are there of choosing the chaser?

9 How can you keep safe, if you need to have a rest in
chasing?

10 If you swop something with a friend, how do you know if
it is forever, or just to borrow?

11 How can you make sure you have good luck?

12 How can you avoid bad luck?

13 Do you have any special sayings if:
   a) someone leaves a door open
   b) someone has a button or zip undone
   c) someone tells you something you've known for ages
   d) someone tells you a very old joke

14 Do you have any special names for animals? e.g. wasp
15 Do you know any special rhymes for choosing chasers for games, for skipping or other games?
16 Do you know any "nonsense" rhymes?

Lexical Index

This is not intended as a subject index, but as an index of every lexical item discussed as such in the body of the text. Foreign words and words from earlier stages of English have been marked with the standard abbreviations. Place-names, surnames, etc. have been capitalized. Dialect and Standard English words are not listed separately – when there is the possibility of confusion as to which word or word-element is being referred to, the Standard English equivalent or some grammatical marker is given. The alphabetical order is absolute, except that Old English "æ" has been treated as "ae" for alphabetical purposes, and *all* words beginning with a "th-" sound, of whatever origin, are listed separately after the letter "t".

192

dudman, 63
Duncan, 55
dunnaken, 71
dunnikin, 71
durns, 50
durs'n, 37
durst not, 37
duru (OE), 78
Dutch yeast, 46
dwarf elder, 110, 111
dyrn (Norw.), 50

ēa (OE), 85
eagle, 85
ear, 21
earn (OE), 85
earth-closet, 71
earwig, 21
east [StE yeast], 21
East Foscote, 81
eat, 34
eaten, 34
Eaton, Castle, 85
Eaton Keynell, 85
Eaton, Water, 85
eaves, 43
-ed, 33
edge, 43
Edward, 55
efes (OE), 43
efeta (OE), 42
egel (OE), 40
elder, 30, 110
eldernberries, 30
elm, 21
embrace, 138
emmet, 42
emmet-but, 77
emmet-knoll, 77
emmet-molds, 89
emmet-tump, 49
empty, 73
-en (adj.suff.), 30
-en (pl.suff.), 25
ened (OE), 96
Enford, 96
enge, 59
English parrot, 131
Ennix Wood, 88
Ennox (Wood), 85, 88
'er, 27
-er, 31
erne, 85

even, 75
evening, 75
evet, 42
excrement, 73

fainites, 67
fains, 67
fairies' thimble, 108
fairy cap, 108
falcon, peregrine, 126
fall, 74
fall of the leaf, 75
fall of the year, 74, 75
fane, 13
farm, 20
farmer, 17, 18
farmyard, 60
Farthing, Stoke, 83
fat [StE vat], 13
February Fill-dyke, 76
feer-, 67
feerin, 67
feering, 67
feign, 67
fellet, 88
fellies, 19
Feltham, 88
Feniscowles, 83
Fenn, 98
Fennisutton, 83
fenny, 83, 98
Fenny Bentley, 83
Fenny Compton, 83
Fenny Drayton, 83
Fennymere, 83
fent, 13
Ferdon, Stoke, 83
field, 44
field bindweed, 105, 115
fifer's dance, 75
fighting cocks, 107
finc (OE), 118
finch, 117, 118
finch, pie, 130
*fink (Gmc.), 118
Finkley, 118
Fittleton, 3, 81
fixen, 13
flagellum (Lat.), 44
flaiel (OF), 44
flail, 44, 45
fledermaus (Ger.), 57
fledged, 59

197

201

203

yellow, 23, 31
yellow stonecrop, 110
yellowy, 31
yelm, 21
Yeo, 85
yerrins, 21
yes, 21
yesterday, 21
Yetton, 85
yiccups, 21
you (disjunctive pron.), 29
yourn, 28
yours, 28

yuckle, 117
yʒeve, (ME), 3

Zeals, 83
zeen, 34
*zheep, 19
zhilling, 17, 19
zhoulder, 19
zhrink, 16
zhugar, 18
zix, 17
Zons Barns, 83, 84